Business Guides on the Go

"Business Guides on the Go" presents cutting-edge insights from practice on particular topics within the fields of business, management, and finance. Written by practitioners and experts in a concise and accessible form the series provides professionals with a general understanding and a first practical approach to latest developments in business strategy, leadership, operations, HR management, innovation and technology management, marketing or digitalization. Students of business administration or management will also benefit from these practical guides for their future occupation/careers.

These Guides suit the needs of today's fast reader.

Sven Reinecke • Laura Johanna Noll

Active Price Management

Be a Price Maker, Not a Price Taker!

Sven Reinecke
Institute for Marketing and
Customer Insight
University of St. Gallen
St. Gallen, Switzerland

Laura Johanna Noll
Institute for Marketing and
Customer Insight
University of St. Gallen
St. Gallen, Switzerland

ISSN 2731-4758 ISSN 2731-4766 (electronic)
Business Guides on the Go
ISBN 978-3-031-42048-1 ISBN 978-3-031-42049-8 (eBook)
https://doi.org/10.1007/978-3-031-42049-8

Translation from the German language edition: "Aktives Preismanagement" by Sven Reinecke and Laura Johanna Noll, © Der/die Herausgeber bzw. der/die Autor(en), exklusiv lizenziert an Springer Fachmedien Wiesbaden GmbH, ein Teil von Springer Nature 2023. Published by Springer Fachmedien Wiesbaden. All Rights Reserved.

© The Editor(s) (if applicable) and The Author(s), under exclusive license to Springer Nature Switzerland AG 2023

This work is subject to copyright. All rights are solely and exclusively licensed by the Publisher, whether the whole or part of the material is concerned, specifically the rights of reprinting, reuse of illustrations, recitation, broadcasting, reproduction on microfilms or in any other physical way, and transmission or information storage and retrieval, electronic adaptation, computer software, or by similar or dissimilar methodology now known or hereafter developed.

The use of general descriptive names, registered names, trademarks, service marks, etc. in this publication does not imply, even in the absence of a specific statement, that such names are exempt from the relevant protective laws and regulations and therefore free for general use.

The publisher, the authors, and the editors are safe to assume that the advice and information in this book are believed to be true and accurate at the date of publication. Neither the publisher nor the authors or the editors give a warranty, expressed or implied, with respect to the material contained herein or for any errors or omissions that may have been made. The publisher remains neutral with regard to jurisdictional claims in published maps and institutional affiliations.

This Springer imprint is published by the registered company Springer Nature Switzerland AG
The registered company address is: Gewerbestrasse 11, 6330 Cham, Switzerland

Paper in this product is recyclable.

Preface

In economics textbooks, the price (P) is always shown on the Y-axis—it is therefore a dependent variable that results from the quantity (Q) offered on the market. Even if this may make sense for the market as a whole, it is nonsense for the individual company. The price must rather be an active variable, which the offering company can and *should* set itself. Based on this decision and the value customers perceive of the overall offer, the quantity that a company can sell in the market is determined.

Benson P. Shapiro formulated it very aptly a long time ago at the Harvard Business School as a call to action for professional management: "Be a price maker, not a price taker." It should not be the case that responsible managers lower the price just to gain market share or an image-boosting customer. After all, price is the customer's consideration for the other three value-creating marketing instruments: product (functional value), communication (emotional value), and distribution (availability).

In this booklet, we show how the "stepchild" in marketing, pricing, can be turned into the marketing instrument that has the most lasting positive influence on the company's profit. It is about active price management. In doing so, we do not aim to publish a comprehensive basic textbook on this topic. Although we present the most important framework conditions and basic principles of price management, we otherwise pick out, without claiming to be complete, those aspects that have proven to be particularly relevant for corporate practice in the context of executive education at the University of St. Gallen (HSG).

Enjoy reading—and thank you for your constructive feedback!

St. Gallen, Switzerland Sven Reinecke
St. Gallen, Switzerland Laura Johanna Noll
12.07.2023

Contents

1 Active Price Management: Fundamentals and Challenges   1
   1.1   Definition of Price Management   1
   1.2   Price Management in the Marketing Mix   2
   1.3   Challenges and Tasks of Price Management   5
   References   6

2 Conditions of Price Management   9
   2.1   The Three Cs of Price Management   9
      2.1.1   Costs   10
      2.1.2   Competition   14
      2.1.3   Customer Benefits   14
   2.2   Digitalization and Price Management   16
   References   18

3 Goals of Price Management   21
   3.1   Quantitative Price Targets   21
   3.2   Qualitative Price Targets   22
   References   25

4 Price Management Strategies — 27
4.1 Pricing Strategies at a Glance — 28
    4.1.1 Premium Price Strategy (Static) — 29
    4.1.2 Price–Quantity Strategy (Static) — 31
    4.1.3 Price Differentiation (Static) — 32
    4.1.4 Skimming Strategy (Dynamic) — 32
    4.1.5 Penetration Strategy (Dynamic) — 32
4.2 Innovative Pricing Models — 33
    4.2.1 Decoy Pricing — 33
    4.2.2 Bundling — 34
    4.2.3 Freemium — 35
    4.2.4 Add-on — 35
    4.2.5 Subscription — 35
    4.2.6 Pay-per-Use — 36
    4.2.7 Flat Rate — 36
    4.2.8 Performance-Based Pricing — 36
    4.2.9 Success-Based Pricing — 37
    4.2.10 Pay-What-You-Want — 37
    4.2.11 Auctioning — 38
    4.2.12 Switching — 38
4.3 Price Differentiation and Variation — 38
    4.3.1 Comparison of Price Differentiation Strategies — 40
    4.3.2 Criteria-Based Price Differentiation — 40
    4.3.3 Self-Selection — 46
References — 48

5 Price Management for Innovations — 51
5.1 Use of Available Market Data — 52
5.2 Customer Survey — 52
    5.2.1 Direct Customer Survey — 53
    5.2.2 Indirect Customer Survey: Conjoint Analysis — 57
5.3 Price Experiments — 60
5.4 Expert Survey/Delphi Method — 60
References — 61

6 Auctions 63
6.1 Significance, Goals, and Fields of Application 63
6.2 Auction Forms 65
6.2.1 One and Two-Sided Auctions 65
6.2.2 Open Auctions 66
6.2.3 Hidden Auctions 68
6.3 Other Design Dimensions 69
References 70

7 Price Management for Business-to-Business Services 71
7.1 Industrial Services 72
7.2 Clearing Approaches 73
7.2.1 Selection 74
7.2.2 Optimize 75
7.2.3 Explain 75
7.2.4 Upgrade 76
7.2.5 Separate 76
7.2.6 Let Choose 77
7.2.7 Transform 77
References 77

8 Conclusion on Active Price Management 79
References 82

References 83

1

Active Price Management: Fundamentals and Challenges

In economics textbooks, the price (P) is always shown on the Y-axis as a dependent variable that results from the number of goods or services offered on the market (Q). Although this makes sense for the market, it is senseless for the individual company. Instead, the price should be an active variable set by the company. Based on the pricing decision and the value of the offering as perceived by customers, the quantity that a company can sell is determined.

Active price management is, therefore, a central and strategic marketing instrument. It involves actively *designing, steering, and developing prices*. Price changes have an immediate effect and are immediately reflected in the company's demand, sales, and profit. While the other instrumental areas *create* value (*value creation*), price *captures* the value of a product or service *(value capture)*.

1.1 Definition of Price Management

According to the St. Gallen management definition (Bleicher 2011, p. 46), the authors understand **price management** as pricing *design, control, and development*. The **price** is the number of monetary units that a consumer must spend for a unit of quantity of a product or service (Simon and Fassnacht 2016, p. 6; c.f. Diller et al. 2021, p. 38). In addition to costs and sales volume, price is the third determinant of profit. It has entrepreneurial significance (Reinecke and Hahn 2003, pp. 335). The price must always be considered in the *price/performance ratio*, i.e., in relation to the performance. It always has two components: a *monetary amount*, or price counter, and *performance*, or price denominator or price reference base (e.g., CHF/piece or Euro/liter). Both components affect the customer's subjective assessment and influence each other: the expected performance (benefit) and the price. To trigger a purchase decision, the net benefit—the difference between benefit and total expenditure, including price—must be positive. Between competing products, customers choose the product or service with the greatest expected net benefit.

1.2 Price Management in the Marketing Mix

Pricing is the moment of truth – all marketing comes to focus in the pricing decision.
   Prof. Raymond Corey, Harvard Business School

The **marketing mix** is the combination of the **four instrumental areas** chosen for a fixed period: *product (product, service, and assortment policy), price management, communication,* and *distribution* (among others Assael 1993; McCarthy 1960; Meffert et al. 2018; Weinhold-Stünzi 1994): These marketing tools are traditionally referred to as the **4 P** (product, price, promotion, and place) (Tomczak et al. 2017).

Price management occupies a **unique position** in the marketing mix: Since the price is the performance of the customer, price management must always be considered in the context of the other marketing instruments (see Fig. 1.1). Problems in price management often have their cause in other instrumental areas (e.g., product quality or distribution). Overall, customers perceive the instruments of the marketing mix in their entirety.

Overall perception of marketing mix instruments—example: Apple Macintosh

1 Active Price Management: Fundamentals and Challenges

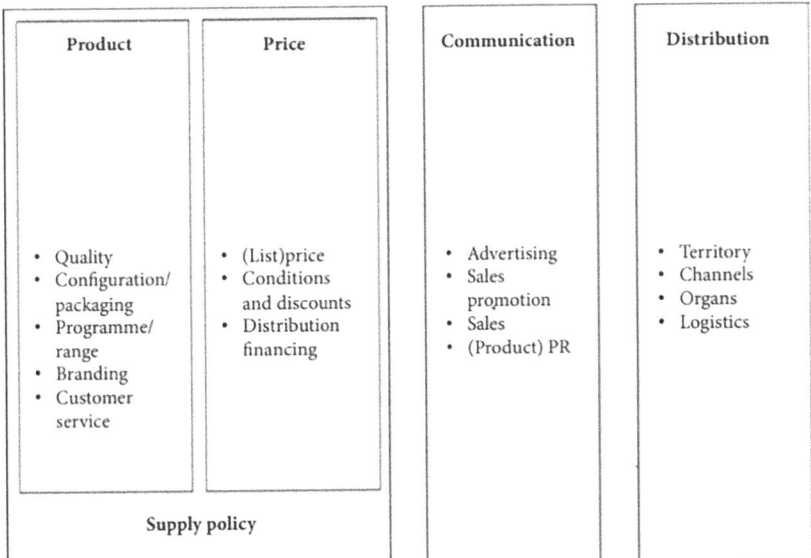

Fig. 1.1 Overview of marketing tools *(Source:* Tomczak et al. 2017, *p. 172)*

> The perceived value of a *Mac* depends not only on the performance, reliability, and quality of the computer but also, for instance, on the brand image (*Apple*), the buying environment (*Apple Store*), and the delivery (e.g., speed and punctuality, unboxing).

Customers make a purchase decision if they expect a personal *gain in value* from the overall perceived offer or service system (Grosse-Oetringhaus 2013; Kotler et al. 2007, pp. 43). From various offers, they choose the offer with the highest personal value gain. The *personal value gain* represents the *difference between the value sum and the cost sum of the offer* (see Fig. 1.2). The marketing instruments significantly influence both sums. The perceived cost sum depends, among other things, on the individual assessment of:

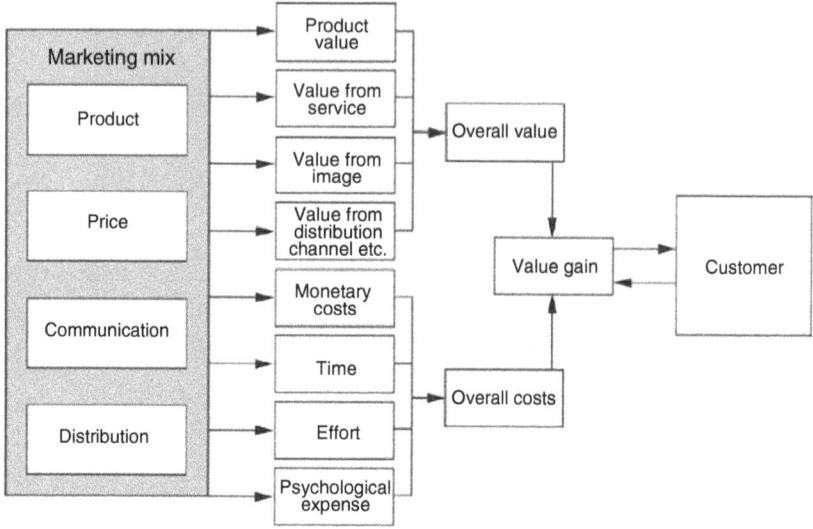

Fig. 1.2 Value gain of customers *(Source:* Tomczak et al. 2017, *p. 174)*

- *Monetary costs* (e.g., leasing offers, discount systems, financing models, or "bait-and-switch" offers)
- *Procurement time and effort* (e.g., self-collection versus delivery, self-configuration versus sales consultation)
- *Physical effort* (e.g., perceived security through warranty services or image through negotiation processes)

Marketing efforts can focus on *customer acquisition* and *customer retention*. For this, *customer satisfaction* is critical: After customers are motivated to buy by a high-value proposition (customer acquisition), the actual value gain ("actual value") must at least match, or exceed, the previously expected value gain ("target value") to ensure customer loyalty (Kotler et al. 2007, pp. 43). This challenge is also central to price management.

1.3 Challenges and Tasks of Price Management

Price management is a core component of marketing strategy. It has a higher and faster impact on profit than any other marketing tool (Herrmann 2003, p. 35; Simon and Fassnacht 2019). Price management offers companies the opportunity to differentiate themselves from the competition (Kim et al. 2009). It directly impacts consumer behavior, helps to identify new business areas, and significantly influences corporate success (Piercy et al. 2010). However, despite very high investments in producing and developing products and services, many products are sold too cheaply (Marn et al. 2003). The prospect theory illustrates the problem of a cheap market introduction (Kahneman and Tversky 1979). According to this theory, subsequent price increases are perceived more strongly than price reductions by the same amount. Therefore, the challenge is to set the "right" price at the outset (Reinecke et al. 2008).

The central *task of price management* is defining and enforcing prices aligned with a company's objectives. Price management occupies a special position within the marketing mix and has three particular features.

1. The price is the **monetary consideration of the customer.** Thus, price management is the counterpart to the other three marketing instruments: While the other instrumental areas *create* value *(value creation)*, the price *captures* the value of a product or service *(value capture)*.
2. Price adjustments elicit an **immediate response from the market.** While adjustments in the other instrumental areas (e.g., in product design, advertising campaigns, or even a change in the distribution system) take a long time, price changes are reflected immediately in the demand and profit of a company.
3. Price management is a **strategic marketing instrument.** Despite its immediate effects, it is not purely tactical or short-term but closely linked to strategic decisions.

The two price functions, acquisitive effect and cost recovery or profit, can conflict. Price management is complex and associated with uncertainty, but at the same time, it has a strong influence on corporate growth and profitability. The impact of price management is already evident in minor price adjustments: for example, a 1% price increase for S&P 1500 companies leads to an average increase in profit of 8% (Marn et al. 2003, p. 29). This leverage effect is not equally high in all industries but is generally considerable. Therefore, the pricing competence of top management is an essential prerequisite for successful price management (Hinterhuber and Liozu 2012).

Pricing decisions—*price changes* for established products and services and *pricing decisions* for new launches—must always be made against the background of the overall marketing mix. The company's cost structure, the industry, the general economic situation, consumers' behavior, and the competition play an important role. However, since the competition can implement price changes quickly, lasting competitive advantages can hardly be achieved with price alone (Simon and Fassnacht 2016, p. 8).

References

Assael, H. (1993). *Marketing principles and strategy*. Thomson Learning.
Bleicher, K. (2011). *Das Konzept integriertes Management: Visionen – Missionen – Programme*. Campus Verlag.
Diller, H., Beinert, M., Ivens, B., & Müller, S. (2021). *Pricing: Prinzipien und Prozesse der betrieblichen Preispolitik* (5th ed.). Kohlhammer.
Grosse-Oetringhaus, W. F. (2013). *Strategische Identität – Orientierung im Wandel: Ganzheitliche Transformation zu Spitzenleistungen*. Springer.
Hermann, A. (2003). Relevanz des Preismanagements für den Unternehmenserfolg. In *Handbuch Preispolitik* (pp. 33–45). Gabler.
Hinterhuber, A., & Liozu, S. (2012). Is it time to rethink your pricing strategy? *MIT Sloan Management Review, 53*(4), 69–77.
Kahneman, D., & Tversky, A. (1979). Prospect theory: An analysis of decision under risk. *Econometrica, 47*(2), 263–292.
Kim, J. Y., Natter, M., & Spann, M. (2009). Pay what you want: A new participative pricing mechanism. *Journal of Marketing, 73*(1), 44–58.

Kotler, P., Keller, K. L., & Bliemel, F. (2007). *Marketing-Management: Strategien für wertschaffendes Handeln* (12th updated and revised edition). Pearson Studies.

Marn, M. V., Roegner, E. V., & Zawada, C. C. (2003). The power of pricing. *The McKinsey Quarterly, 2003*(1), 26–36.

McCarthy, E. J. (1960). *Basic marketing: A managerial approach*. Homewood.

Meffert, H., Burmann, C., Kirchgeorg, M., & Eisenbeiss, M. (2018). *Marketing: Grundlagen marktorientierter Unternehmensführung Konzepte – Instrumente – Praxisbeispiele*. Springer.

Piercy, N. F., Cravens, D. W., & Lane, N. (2010). Thinking strategically about pricing decisions. *The Journal of Business Strategy, 31*(5), 38–48.

Reinecke, S., & Hahn, S. (2003). Preisplanung. In H. Diller & A. Herrmann (Eds.), *Handbuch Preispolitik* (pp. 333–355). Springer.

Reinecke, S., Fischer, P. M., & Mühlmeier, S. (2008). Aktuelle Herausforderungen für das Preiscontrolling. *Controlling & Management, 52*(2), 112–114.

Simon, H., & Fassnacht, M. (2016). *Preismanagement: Strategie – Analyse – Entscheidung – Umsetzung* (4th ed.). Springer.

Simon, H., & Fassnacht, M. (2019). *Price management: Strategy – analysis – decision – implementation*. Springer.

Tomczak, T., Reinecke, S., & Kuss, A. (2017). *Strategic marketing: Market-oriented corporate and business unit planning*. Springer.

Weinhold-Stünzi, H. (1994). *Marketing in 20 Lektionen*. Fachmed

2

Conditions of Price Management

Price management focuses on three central determinants: costs, competition, and customer benefits (three Cs). Accordingly, a distinction is traditionally made between cost- and company-oriented, competition-oriented, and customer-oriented determinants and procedures of price management (Hinterhuber 2008; Hinterhuber and Liozu 2012; Indounas 2009).

2.1 The Three Cs of Price Management

The three central determinants of price management are the ***three Cs: costs, competition, and customer value*** (see Fig. 2.1): the *costs* of the supplier, the behavior and structure of the *competition*, and the value perception and behavior of the *customers* (Diller et al. 2021, pp. 158; Tucker 1966, p. 19). Often, only costs, competitive prices, or rules of thumb are considered in price management (Breidert et al. 2006; Wübker 2006, p. 37). Instead, it would be more customer-oriented to focus on willingness to pay. The latter is a crucial factor in the price-sales function.

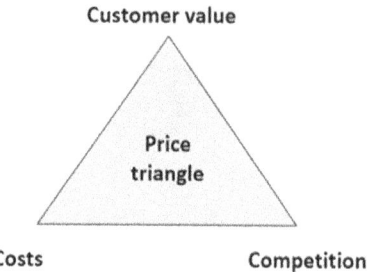

Fig. 2.1 Three Cs of price management *(Source: Own illustration adapted from Reinecke and Hahn 2003)*

2.1.1 Costs

Price management often focuses on costs since products and services can only be offered long-term if proportional (or variable) and fixed costs (full cost accounting) are covered. Accordingly, the cost-based method of price management is based on existing data and considers costs for research, material, production, distribution, and marketing (Hinterhuber and Liozu 2012; Hinterhuber and Bertini 2011).

The fixed costs must be covered or exceeded since they cannot be influenced or reduced in the short term. The proportional costs must be covered in the short term (unit costing). They form a certain price floor (Ingenbleek et al. 2003). This is because a contribution margin is only generated if the price is higher than the unit costs. Two methods of price management are possible: *retrograde calculation* and *progressive calculation*. Retrograde calculation (or experience costing) checks the actual selling price for profitability. Progressive calculation (or overhead costing) adds a profit markup to the cost of a product or service. This method is also called cost-plus calculation and is common in practice (Hinterhuber and Liozu 2012). However, if customers have a high willingness to pay, high-profit potentials can be given away, while other offers become significantly too expensive from the customer's point of view.

The advantage of *cost- and company-oriented methods* is the availability of the required data in the cost accounting system (Hinterhuber and Liozu 2012; Hinterhuber and Bertini 2011). However, the allocation to products and services is often a challenge (Hinterhuber and Liozu 2012;

Shipley and Jobber 2001). Also, customers and the competition are neglected. Therefore, pricing should not be based only on product coverage contributions but also on customers' contribution margins (e.g., special prices in key account management).

In addition, it is necessary to compare own and third-party offerings and product lines. For example, the *Volkswagen Group* must consider prices and market performances of comparable models (*Volkswagen, Skoda,* etc.). Other and own brand or product lines can also influence the pricing procedure. For example, *Snickers* and *Mars* prices need to be aligned to avoid cannibalization and substitution effects.

In particular, the costs must be considered when **setting the conditions**. This involves deviations from so-called normal or list prices. Typical conditions are *discounts* (e.g., price reductions under certain conditions, e.g., minimum quantities), *bonuses* (e.g., yearly rebates according to annual sales), cash discounts (e.g., percentage deductions for cash or immediate payment), *delivery terms* (e.g., allocation of transport and insurance costs), and *payment terms* (e.g., financing and leasing offers). Examples of discounts are shown in Table 2.1 (supplemented based on Paul and Colleagues, Vienna):

In the case of price reductions, it should be noted that a significant increase in sales is required to compensate for the lost contribution margins (see Fig. 2.2).

There is a risk of a dangerous price waterfall if numerous parties in the company are involved in price management and grant different discounts, which accumulate (see Fig. 2.3). The problem is inadequate price organization: those involved in the same company often know too little about each other and each grant a few percentage points discounts, e.g., the salesforce offers a 5% volume discount, key account management a 5% special customer discount, logistics eliminates freight costs, accounting grants a 2% cash discount, and so on. The blue graphic in Fig. 2.3 (Marn et al. 2003, p. 31) illustrates the effects: a standard list price of 100 results in a final net price of only 50. As the yellow graph shows, this also leads to different customers paying different prices, which is particularly problematic when less profitable customers profit more than profitable customers. For price fairness, this should be avoided if an exchange between these customers is possible.

Table 2.1 Selected discount types *(Source: Supplemented selection based on Paul and Colleagues, Vienna)*

Selected discount types		
Action discount	Annual bonus	Window discount
Anti-campaign discount	Anniversary discount	Service discount
Order size discount	Carton discount	Discount
Exhibition discount	Core assortment discount	Immediate discount
Stock exchange discount	Loading discount	Instant account
Permanent low-price discount	Stock discount	Social media discount
Display discount	List fee	Increase discount
Event discount	Quantity discount	Instant discount
Action discount	Birthday discount	Newsletter discount
Facebook discount	Natural discount	Loyalty discount
Newsletter discount	Newsletter discount	Value date discount
Birthday discount	Package bonus	Sales promotion discount
Handout discount	Pallet discount	Full-range discount
House bonus	Quarterly bonus	Advance discount
Collection discount	Shelf rental	Advertising allowance
Internet discount	Seasonal discount	Target achievement bonus

In addition, the short- and long-term effects of discounts differ between first-time and existing customers (Anderson and Simester 2004): The short-term effect of promotion can be positive for first-time and existing customers (a larger order quantity may even overcompensate the price reduction), but the long-term effect of promotion is often negative because, as a result of the promotion, consumption is adapted to the company's promotion cycle (cf. Sun 2005, p. 430). For example, customers only buy their preferred detergent when it is currently on special offer. In this case, promotions also have a long-term negative impact on the enforcement of high prices and the company's success. For first-time customers, discounts may also have a positive long-term effect, for example, due to little experience with the company (Anderson and Simester 2004).

2 Conditions of Price Management

Discount	Contribution margin as a percentage of the sales price									
	2%	3%	4%	5%	10%	15%	20%	25%	30%	35%	40%
1%	100.0	50.0	33.3	25.0	11.1	7.1	5.3	4.2	3.4	2.9	2.6
2%		200.0	100.0	66.6	25.0	15.4	11.1	8.7	7.1	6.1	5.3
3%			300.0	150.0	42.8	25.0	17.6	13.6	11.1	9.4	8.1
4%				400.0	66.6	36.4	25.0	19.0	15.4	12.9	11.1
5%					100.0	50.0	33.3	25.0	20.0	16.7	14.3
6%					150.0	66.7	42.9	31.6	25.0	20.7	17.6
7%					233.3	87.5	53.8	38.9	30.4	25.0	21.2
8%					400.0	114.3	66.7	47.1	36.4	29.8	25.0
9%					900.0	150.0	81.8	56.3	42.9	34.6	29.0
10%						200.0	100.0	66.7	50.0	40.0	33.3
15%							300.0	150.0	100.0	75.0	60.0
20%								400.0	200.0	133.3	100.0
25%									500.0	250.0	166.7
30%										600.0	300.0
35%											700.0

Fig. 2.2 Necessary increase in sales to compensate for price reductions *(Source: Own illustration based on* Brühwiler 1989*)*

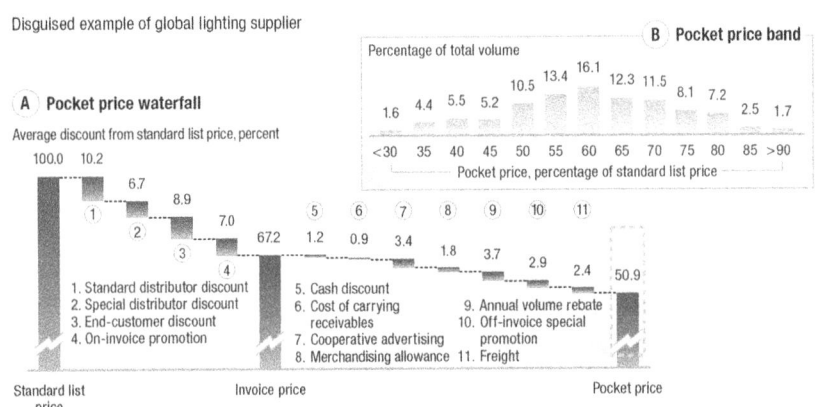

Fig. 2.3 Money in your pocket *(Marn et al. 2003, p. 31, Copyright (c) 2023 McKinsey & Company. All rights reserved. Reprinted by permission)*

2.1.2 Competition

The structure and behavior of the competition also play a central role in price management. Accordingly, the competition-based method of price management considers competitors' products, services, and behavior (Hinterhuber 2008; Hinterhuber and Liozu 2012). The reactions of the competition must be considered, especially in case of low competition (e.g., in a duopoly or oligopoly) or for products without a significant competitive advantage (Ingenbleek et al. 2003; Hinterhuber 2008).

To this end, *competitive price management methods* are often chosen to define *strategic prices*. One example of *competitive price management* is *street-level pricing*. Here, prices are based on the market level, and an average price or market price is set. Another option is *price matching*. Here, prices are based on direct competition. For instance, prices are aligned between two gas stations located in the same city. Market share can be lost if the competition does not follow suit with price increases. If competitors follow suit in cutting prices, the general price level may fall, leading to a *"race to the bottom,"* often observed in digital competition.

In some cases, it appears necessary to set a "strategic" price oriented to the competition, e.g., if central industrial customers with a vital image function are to be won or retained. However, the associated prices often do not cover a company's (full) costs and are thus questionable from a business management point of view (Shipley and Jobber 2001). Furthermore, as with cost-based methods, customer needs are neglected (Amaral and Guerreiro 2019; Kienzler 2018). On the other hand, independence from the competition increases with the heterogeneity between competing companies. A *niche strategy*, for example, may deliberately gear toward differentiation, while in *adaptation strategy*, all companies are oriented toward a "price leader" (Siems 2009, p. 77).

2.1.3 Customer Benefits

Active price management focuses on customers' willingness to pay to avoid profit losses from cost-plus pricing. **Value pricing** is recommended to exploit willingness to pay optimally. Here, the focus is not on the company's costs but individual customer value (Ingenbleek 2007, 2014). Active price management is driven by demand (Hinterhuber 2008; Nagle et al. 2011). Customer-centric approaches enable companies to achieve high prices by increasing perceived customer value and thus increasing willingness to pay (Hinterhuber and Liozu 2012). In addition, they benefit company profitability in the long term (Hinterhuber 2008; Nagle et al. 2011).

The so-called *price elasticity* provides information on the direction and extent of the expected demand change in the event of a price change. It is the product of the relative change in sales in % and the relative change in price in %:

$$Price\ elasticity = \frac{\%change\ in\ quantity\ demanded}{\%change\ in\ price}$$

Price elasticity depends, among other things, on customers' knowledge of prices, customer relations, and the uniqueness, image, and substitutability of a product. Therefore, the importance of price—and thus price elasticity—increases, for example, together with customers' price knowledge (e.g., for butter, milk, and gasoline) (Shapiro 1968) and with the substitutability of a product (e.g., generic drugs). In contrast, price elasticity decreases with the increasing importance of image and customer relations and the uniqueness of a product or service (Siems 2009, p. 100, 392). Since price elasticity depends on various factors, the function between price and sales can be very different: *linear, multiplicative, double-curved,* or *logistic* (e.g., Diller et al. 2021, pp. 193). This function is called the *price-sales function.* Figure 2.4 visualizes selected variants of the *price-sales function.* As in business administration, the price is plotted on the x-axis as an independent, active, and shapeable variable.

In practice, determining price elasticity, customer value, and willingness to pay is challenging, as well as communicating product value (Hinterhuber 2008; Hinterhuber and Bertini 2011; Michel and Pfäffli 2013).

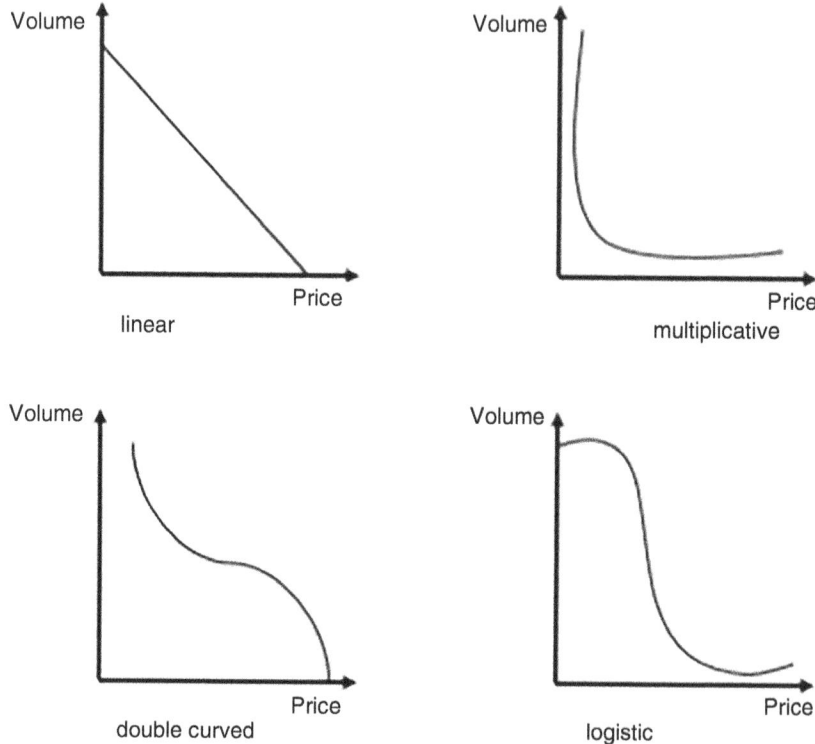

Fig. 2.4 Selected variants of the price-sales function *(Source: Own illustration based on Diller et al. 2021, p. 204)*

2.2 Digitalization and Price Management

Digitalization increases market transparency. Information on products and services is available regardless of time and place (e.g., 24 hours a day, 7 days a week, worldwide), and information and transaction costs are reduced. As a result, price adjustments can be made more quickly and more frequently. Price experiments and auctions can be conducted more easily online. Also, customers are integrated into the communication and creation process, which leads to personalized products and services (e.g., one-to-one marketing, customizing) and multimedia offerings (including audio, video, text, images, 3D prints) (Tomczak et al. 2014, p. 198).

Digitalization increases the risk of "race-to-the-bottom" pricing due to automation. The principle of *"the winner takes it all"* often applies. Overall, the effects of digitalization on the *three Cs* are as follows (see Table 2.2):

On the *cost side,* digitalization enables better capacity utilization. Discounters benefit from the improved reach and network effects. In addition, premium prices can be enforced for specialties ("longtail" of the assortment). Variable costs are often close to zero, so economies of scale have a substantial impact.

Digitalization increases price transparency and thus the *intensity of competition*. It also enables a (faster) reaction to competitor prices, which means that the competition's countermeasures must be considered. Particularly, game-theoretical considerations become relevant. Also, the Internet makes fraudulent (low-price) offers more difficult because provider ratings and social media reveal them immediately.

To summarize, digitalization enables greater precision in price management; in particular, *customer values* can be better assessed. Entirely new forms of customer segmentation emerge: For example, users are offered different prices depending on the device they use. Likewise, it is possible to charge higher prices if the customer uses an *Apple* device

Table 2.2 Impact of digitalization on costs, competition, and customer benefits *(Source: Own presentation)*

Costs	Competition	Customer benefits
• "Longtail" enables premium prices for specialties • Improved reach and network effects for discounters • Better capacity utilization possible • **Variable costs = zero**	• Increased **price transparency** • (Faster) reaction to competitive prices (game theory) • "Cheating" not possible/meaningful due to social media and ratings	• **Precision**: Faster detection of price elasticity • New forms of **customer segmentation** (e.g., device, IP address, cookies, browser, click behavior) • Lower price elasticity due to "safety" of good ratings
• **Price adjustment** possible more **quickly** and more frequently (risk: race to the bottom) • Price experiments possible • Increased use of **auctions**		

because *Apple* users are assumed to have a higher willingness to pay. Similarly, different prices are possible depending on IP address (international price differentiation!), cookies, browser usage, and previous search and click behavior. Likewise, price-sensitive customers who are redirected from a price comparison portal are offered lower prices than those who visit a website directly (e.g., device, IP address, cookies, browser, click behavior). The positive evaluation of some providers by many customers leads to a reduction in price elasticity due to higher customer safety.

References

Amaral, J. V., & Guerreiro, R. (2019). Factors explaining a cost-based pricing essence. *Journal of Business & Industrial Marketing, 34*(8), 1850–1865.

Anderson, E. T., & Simester, D. I. (2004). Long-run effects of promotion depth on new versus established customers: Three field studies. *Marketing Science, 23*(1), 4–20.

Breidert, C., Hahsler, M., & Reutterer, T. (2006). A review of methods for measuring willingness-to-pay. *Innovative Marketing, 2*(4), 8–32.

Brühwiler, C. (1989). *Der ruinöse Preiskampf: Marketinglösungen bei übersteigertem Wettbewerb*. Dissertation, University of St. Gallen.

Diller, H., Beinert, M., Ivens, B., & Müller, S. (2021). *Pricing: Prinzipien und Prozesse der betrieblichen Preispolitik* (5th ed.). Kohlhammer.

Hinterhuber, A. (2008). Customer value-based pricing strategies: Why companies resist. *Journal of Business Strategy, 29*(4), 41–50.

Hinterhuber, A., & Bertini, M. (2011). Profiting when customers choose value over price. *Business Strategy Review, 22*(1), 46–49.

Hinterhuber, A., & Liozu, S. (2012). Is it time to rethink your pricing strategy? *MIT Sloan Management Review, 53*(4), 69–77.

Indounas, K. A. (2009). Successful industrial service pricing. *Journal of Business & Industrial Marketing, 24*(2), 86–97.

Ingenbleek, P. T. (2007). Value-informed pricing in its organizational context: Literature review, conceptual framework, and directions for future research. *Journal of Product & Brand Management, 16*(7), 441–458.

Ingenbleek, P. T. (2014). The theoretical foundations of value-informed pricing in the service-dominant logic of marketing. *Management Decision, 52*(1), 33–53.

Ingenbleek, P. T., Debruyne, M., Frambach, R. T., & Verhallen, T. M. (2003). Successful new product pricing practices: A contingency approach. *Marketing Letters, 14*(4), 289–305.

Kienzler, 2018: Value-based pricing and cognitive biases: An overview for business markets. *Industrial Marketing Management, 68*(1), 86–94.

Marn, M. V., Roegner, E. V., & Zawada, C. C. (2003). The power of pricing. *The McKinsey Quarterly, 2003*(1), 26–36.

Michel, S., & Pfäffli, P. (2013). Obstacles to implementing value-based pricing. *Perspectives for Managers, 185*, 1–4.

Nagle, T. T., Hogan, J., & Zale, J. (2011). *The strategy and tactics of pricing: A guide to growing more profitably*. Prentice Hall.

Reinecke, S., & Hahn, S. (2003). Preisplanung. In H. Diller & A. Herrmann (Eds.), *Handbuch Preispolitik* (pp. 333–355). Springer.

Shapiro, B. P. (1968). Psychology of pricing. *Harvard Business Review, 46*(4), 14.

Shipley, D., & Jobber, D. (2001). Integrative pricing via the pricing wheel. *Industrial Marketing Management, 30*(3), 301–314.

Siems, F. (2009). *Preismanagement: Konzepte – Strategien – Instrumente*. Vahlens Handbücher.

Sun, B. (2005). Promotion effect on endogenous consumption. *Marketing Science, 24*(3), 430–443.

Tomczak, T., Kuss, A., & Reinecke, S. (2014). *Marketingplanung*. Springer Gabler.

Tucker, S. A. (1966). *Pricing for higher profit: Criteria, methods, applications*. McGraw-Hill.

Wübker, S. (2006). *Power Pricing für Banken: Wege aus der Ertragskrise*. Campus.

3

Goals of Price Management

In principle, the goals of price management should be known to everyone in the company involved in price decision-making and implementation (Monroe 2003, pp. 433). They must be considered in the context of overall marketing and oriented to a company's marketing or *positioning strategy*. Common positioning strategies are *higher price* through better performance (or benefits) and non-price instruments or *lower* price through lower costs for the same performance (similar in Simon and Fassnacht 2016, pp. 47). In addition, different *price targets* must be considered for different offerings and customer groups (for more details, see Diller et al. 2021, pp. 130). All price targets are interdependent and must be understood as a target system. Overall, quantitative and qualitative *price targets* are distinguished (Reinecke and Hahn 2003, pp. 341).

3.1 Quantitative Price Targets

Quantitative price targets are

1. *Profit* and *profitability*
2. *Growth*

3. *Safety* (risk reduction)

Profit and profitability are common price targets. In the long term, absolute profit and relative profitability are necessary conditions for economic activity (see in particular Simon 2020). Nevertheless, these quantitative targets are often neglected due to short-term considerations.

Corporate growth is also a common price target. Against this background, revenue or sales targets can be defined. One target is to increase market share. Particularly in new, growing markets, growth, sales, and market share are prioritized. These targets are frequently a priority for listed companies.

Another price target is entrepreneurial *security* (Becker 2019, pp. 16). It can be ensured, for example, by minimizing risk. As a rule, owners of family businesses attach more importance to security (and profitability) than to rapid growth. One reason is that they cannot finance faster growth and avoid expanding debt financing for risk considerations. Family businesses often attach great importance to independence from banks.

On the one hand, the weighting of quantitative price targets depends on the company-specific situation (e.g., legal form and ownership structure) and risk appetite. On the other hand, industry-, company-, and product-specific must be considered.

Overall, quantitative price targets must be set against the background of the positioning strategy addressed above and specified in terms of services, customers, sales, and contribution margins.

In practice, there can be a large discrepancy between the actual and the subjectively perceived price. However, only the subjectively perceived price is decisive for purchasing (Schindler 1998, p. 3). Hence, qualitative price targets must be defined in addition to quantitative targets.

3.2　Qualitative Price Targets

Qualitative price targets are (see, e.g., Diller et al. 2021 pp. 130):

1. *Inexpensiveness*
2. *Value for money*

3. *Price fairness*
4. *Price satisfaction*
5. *Price confidence*

Qualitative price targets depend on the subjective perception of customers and reflect the price image. The customer relationship is decisive: Price satisfaction and price trust are central in long-term (e.g., contractual) relationships. Price favorability may be sufficient for pure (e.g., one-time) transactions.

Inexpensiveness means that the absolute price level is assessed in relation to competing services or other reference prices such as subjective price thresholds (e.g., €1/L) (Zielke 2007), independent from the price–performance ratio. This kind of price cheapness may be sufficient for pure (e.g., one-time) transactions if caused by price intransparency. In addition, competitors can be deterred from entering the market, for example, if the company signalizes a willingness to fight (Belz and Schindler 1994).

Value for money refers to the subjectively perceived price–performance ratio. The term underscores the dependence of price on individual p: Due to different customer needs and their weighting, different customers assess the price worthiness of the same offer differently (Tomczak et al. 2018, p. 182).

Price fairness refers to the perceived fairness of the price from the customer's perspective (Bolton et al. 2003; Diller 2008). The term suggests that the motives behind price differentiation and changes must be comprehensible to customers (Siems 2009, pp. 246). From the customer's point of view, justified reasons (higher costs, new needs, capacity utilization) or unjustified motives (exploitation of market power and customer dependency) determine perceived price fairness and thus (re)purchasing behavior. It is also essential to know how the price is created or calculated and what prices other customers pay for comparable offerings (Bolton et al. 2003). If different prices are paid for the same or a comparable service, customers may feel unfairly treated (Frey and Pommerehne 1993; Michel and Pfäffli 2013). This can negatively affect customer behavior (Michel and Pfäffli 2013; Xia et al. 2004). Whether prices are perceived as fair depends on whether they are consistent, are honest, are reliable, or can be influenced, and whether price managers are opportunistic (Diller 2008, pp. 354; Tomczak et al. 2018, p. 235).

The issue of *price fairness* has gained in importance (Xia et al. 2004): In practice, there have been increasing public debates about the ethical propriety of price increases, especially when they have been introduced despite rising profits, as was the case with *Deutsche Bahn* or *E.ON*. In theory, the effects of price fairness on consumer behavior and corporate performance are studied in terms of their statistical significance. Different studies (Bolton et al. 2003; Gronholdt et al. 2000; Hermann et al. 2007; Konuk 2018; Malc et al. 2021; Maxwell 2002) have shown that perceived price fairness influences willingness to pay, customer satisfaction, and customer loyalty. *Price transparency* is essential for complex purchases and in case of price increases (Hermann et al. 2007). It increases perceived price fairness and price acceptance. Finally, companies need to ensure fair price management, especially during economic crises. If they prioritize short-term revenue gains during this time, long-term corporate profitability can be harmed (Hermann et al. 2007).

> **Lack of price fairness—example: Coca-Cola Value Pricing**

> *For a while, Coca-Cola* varied the prices of beverage vending machines depending on the outside temperature: as the temperature rose, so did the price. However, the press soon put pressure on *Coca-Cola* due to the lack of *price fairness*, so after a short time, the company refrained from this pricing strategy (Dixit et al. 2005).

The above qualitative price objectives are reflected in price satisfaction or price trust (Diller et al. 2021; Siems 2009). *Price satisfaction* describes the correspondence between subjective price expectations and subjective price experience. *Price confidence* refers to individual trust in the affordability, price worthiness, and price fairness of a product or service (Siems 2009, pp. 246; Tomczak et al. 2018, p. 235).

References

Becker, J. (2019). *Marketing-Konzeption: Grundlagen des zielstrategischen und operativen Marketing-Managements*. Vahlen.
Belz, C., & Schindler, H. (1994). Markeintritt des Mediamarkts in die Schweiz. In C. Belz & T. Tomczak (Eds.), *Preisagressive Fachmärkte – Revolution im schweizerischen Einzelhandel* (pp. 14–39). Research Institute for Sales and Trade.
Bolton, L. E., Warlop, L., & Alba, J. W. (2003). Consumer perceptions of price (un)fairness. *Journal of Consumer Research, 29*(4), 474–491.
Diller, H. (2008). Price fairness. *Journal of Product & Brand Management, 17*(5), 353–355.
Diller, H., Beinert, M., Ivens, B., & Müller, S. (2021). *Pricing: Prinzipien und Prozesse der betrieblichen Preispolitik* (5th ed.). Kohlhammer.
Dixit, A., Braunsberger, K., Zinkhan, G. M., & Pan, Y. (2005). Information technology: Enhanced pricing strategies: Managerial and public policy implications. *Journal of Business Research, 58*(9), 1169–1177.
Frey, B. S., & Pommerehne, W. W. (1993). On the fairness of pricing – An empirical survey among the general population. *Journal of Economic Behavior & Organization, 20*(3), 295–307.
Gronholdt, L., Martensen, A., & Kristensen, K. (2000). The relationship between customer satisfaction and loyalty: Cross-industry differences. *Total Quality Management, 11*(4–6), 509–514.
Hermann, A., Xia, L., Monroe, K. B., & Huber, K. (2007). The influence of price fairness on customer satisfaction: An empirical test in the context of automobile purchases. *Journal of Product & Brand Management, 16*(1), 49–58.
Konuk, F. A. (2018). Price fairness, satisfaction, and trust as antecedents of purchase intentions toward organic food. *Journal of Consumer Behavior, 17*(2), 141–148.
Malc, D., Selinšek, A., Dlačić, J., & Milfelner, B. (2021). Exploring the emotional side of price fairness perceptions and its consequences. *Economic Research, 34*(1), 1931–1948.
Maxwell, S. (2002). Rule-based price fairness and its effect on willingness to purchase. *Journal of Economic Psychology, 23*(2), 191–212.
Michel, S., & Pfäffli, P. (2013). Obstacles to implementing value-based pricing. *Perspectives for Managers, 185*, 1–4.
Monroe, K. B. (2003). *Pricing-making profitable decisions* (3rd ed.). McGraw Hill/Irwin.

Reinecke, S., & Hahn, S. (2003). Preisplanung. In H. Diller & A. Herrmann (Eds.), *Handbuch Preispolitik* (pp. 333–355). Springer.
Schindler, H. (1998). *Marktorientiertes Preismanagement*. Schindler.
Siems, F. (2009). *Preismanagement: Konzepte – Strategien – Instrumente*. Vahlens Handbücher.
Simon, H., & Fassnacht, M. (2016). *Preismanagement: Strategie – Analyse – Entscheidung – Umsetzung* (4th ed.). Springer.
Simon, H. (2020). *Am Gewinn ist noch keine Firma kaputt gegangen*. Campus.
Tomczak, T., Reinecke, S., & Kuss, A. (2018): *Strategic Marketing. Market-Oriented Corporate and Business-Unit Planning*. Springer-Gabler.
Xia, L., Monroe, K. B., & Cox, J. L. (2004). The Price is Unfair! A conceptual framework of price fairness perceptions. *Journal of Marketing, 68*(4), 1–15.
Zielke, S. (2007). Bestimmungsfaktoren der Preisfairness von Lebensmitteldiscountern. *Marketing Review St. Gallen, 24*(4), 17–20.

4

Price Management Strategies

Generally, static and dynamic price management strategies are distinguished.

Static price management bases a price decision at a *fixed point in time*. It fixes a price position for the long term. No price changes are expected over time. A typical example is the high prices for luxury goods. Dynamic price management makes price decisions over *a longer period of time* (see also Siems 2009, pp. 162). Over time, price changes are expected. Dynamic price management is particularly useful when new offerings are introduced and when the price affects profits with a time lag. Important examples of time-delayed demand effects are *carry-over effects* (when repeat purchases are expected at a later stage) and *price change effects* (when customers are oriented to earlier prices) (Kucher 1985, pp. 88, Simon 1979, pp. 415). In such cases, there is a connection between the demand of several periods, and a change in price elasticity in the life cycle is possible. Other determinants of dynamic price management are *economies of scale* and *experience curves*.

Throughout digitalization, the possibilities of dynamic price management have increased. For example, online—often without customers' knowledge—prices differ depending on the data collected. For example, browser, search history, or click and conversation rates provide clues about individual decision-making behavior.

4.1 Pricing Strategies at a Glance

Common strategies of *static price management* are

1. Premium price strategy
2. Price–quantity strategy
3. Price differentiation

Typical strategies of *dynamic price management* are

4. Skimming strategy
5. Penetration strategy

Fig. 4.1 visualizes these strategies. It depicts price (on the X-axis) as a function of time (on the Y-axis). In addition, the figure shows a sixth

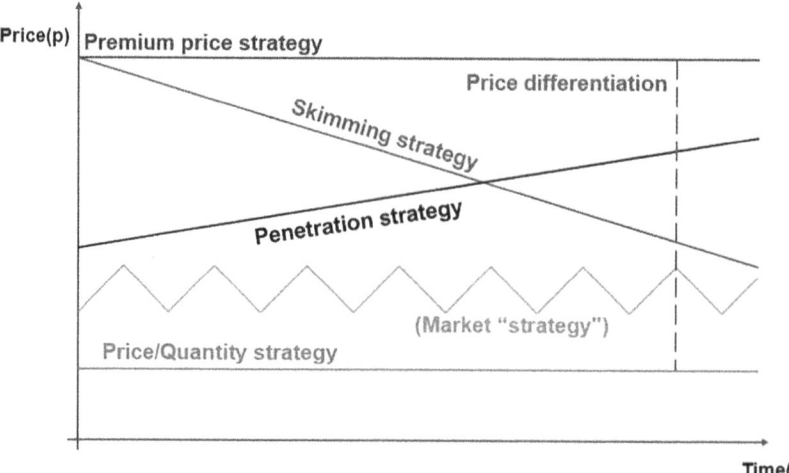

Fig. 4.1 Pricing strategies *(Source: Own illustration closely based on P. Möller, Bayer Crop Science)*

strategy: the market "strategy." Strategy is in quotation marks because the reaction to competitor prices is purely tactical and not an actual strategy. For this reason, there can be no talk of *active* price management. The five typical static and dynamic price management strategies are presented in the following subsections.

4.1.1 Premium Price Strategy (Static)

The premium price strategy follows the principles of a *value-added pricing strategy*. It focuses on the **consistent consideration principle** (quid pro quo). This principle is "*Be a Price Maker, Not a Price Taker*" (Shapiro 2003): Accordingly, companies must

(a) *Create customer value*
(b) *Focus on customer groups that appreciate your values*
(c) *Be different*
(d) *Align prices with benefits*
(e) *Be reliable and consistent*

(a) **Create customer value**

Companies must create a unique customer value. Customer value is defined here as the net value from the customer's point of view. It represents the difference between the individual value and the individual cost. The conceptual value equation is (with best thanks to Steffen Hahn):

$$\text{Net value from the customer's point of view} =$$
$$\textbf{Value}\left(a^* \text{ functional} + b^* \text{ emotional} + c^* \text{ aesthetic} + \ldots\right)$$
$$-\textbf{Cost}\left(x^* \text{ price} + z^* \text{ effort} + w^* \text{ risk} + \ldots\right)$$

The value reflects the subjectively perceived value, which can be functional, emotional, or aesthetic. In addition to price, costs include other factors such as effort and risk. For example, the comparatively low effort associated with a booking on *Booking.com* or an order on *Amazon* (e.g., through time savings and stored payment and delivery information) increases willingness to pay. *Thermomix* offers another example of a unique customer value. Through digitalization, customers receive an exceptionally high functional value and profit from a community effect. In addition, they benefit, e.g., from the aesthetic value of the design and the symbolic value of the original or its popularity.

(b) *Focus on customer groups that appreciate your value*

Companies must focus on customers who appreciate the value of their product or service. If customers value the offer, they are also prepared to pay a high ("good") price. For example, some customers are willing to pay $5 for *Davidoff* matches. Customers who value the offer less will always look for special offers and want to pay low ("bad") prices, regardless of the quality.

When optimizing price management, companies often try to adjust pricing, especially for those customer groups that are not currently profitable. Occasionally, it would be more purposeful to ask why particularly profitable customer groups pay a relatively high price. If necessary, it is possible to increase the profitability of these customer relationships with the help of active price management.

(c) *Be different*

Companies should strive to differentiate their offerings. After all, no one buys an identical and thus interchangeable service from another supplier at a higher price. For example, a *Portland cement* specified according to DIN cannot be sold at a higher price on the stock exchange without any performance differentiation. Nor can an interchangeable standard product be sold on *eBay* at a higher price than the market price.

One way of differentiating is the brand: *NutraSweet*, for example, is the sweetener *aspartame,* but it fetches a significantly higher price as a branded product. Also, an *Apple* computer is not a standard PC.

(d) *Align prices with benefits*

One possibility of the premium price strategy is to orient prices to customer benefits. For example, an American IT service company introduced a special remuneration and incentive system vis-à-vis a wholesale company. The service company was able to charge a higher price for a new logistics system the lower the number of incorrect deliveries, the average inventory, and the number of complaints from retailers, and the higher the employee productivity. The measures included bonuses for target achievement and a share of the IT service company if the wholesale company was successful. The client company took little risk because it only had to pay in case of success. As a result, customer satisfaction and company performance increased significantly (Reinecke 1996; Steinert-Threkeld 1993).

(e) *Be reliable and consistent*

Companies must be reliable and consistent. Sudden and drastic special offers can jeopardize customers' price confidence. If a company pursues a strategy of not granting discounts as a matter of principle, this also means that it must be consistent in its price implementation. In other words, it is occasionally necessary not to concede a discount in specific individual cases to operate more successfully in the long term.

4.1.2 Price–Quantity Strategy (Static)

In the *price-volume strategy* or discount strategy, price management becomes the focus of marketing. The aim is to be perceived as *more favorable* than the competition because low prices motivate people to buy. This strategy is primarily pursued by larger companies and the retail sector, where high sales volumes, low-cost production, and rationalization are possible (Froböse 2016, pp. 73). However, low prices must be compensated by higher sales volumes. Therefore, the term "price/quantity strategy" is deliberately chosen instead of "low-price strategy."

In the long term, a successful *price/quantity strategy* requires that the company is a cost leader. Otherwise, the competition can always undercut the offer. One challenge with this strategy is that the position "low-priced" is often already occupied. For example, not all companies can credibly take on the role of a *Lidl*, *Aldi*, or *Denner in retail*.

4.1.3 Price Differentiation (Static)

Companies can increase their contribution margin through price differentiation by separating different customer segments ("fencing"). In doing so, the willingness to pay in the respective segments is optimally skimmed off. Different prices are accepted, e.g., in the case of subjective product or performance assessment, individual purchasing power, and different price elasticities. Price differentiation is discussed in detail in *Sect. 4.3*.

4.1.4 Skimming Strategy (Dynamic)

The *skimming strategy* is recommended for products with a high innovative capacity and low short-term price elasticity. The skimming strategy (derived from "skimming off cream") introduces the new offer at a relatively high price and gradually reduces it over time (Marburger 2012). It prioritizes short-term profits and cost recovery (Simon and Fassnacht 2016, pp. 301). The high launch price signals quality and enables price reductions over time. In the short term, high profits are generated for newly introduced services and innovations. The competitive risk is reduced in the long term, and willingness to pay is gradually skimmed off (Simon and Fassnacht 2016, p. 304). The strategy is particularly suitable for innovative industries (e.g., automotive or electronics) and products (e.g., *Apple*) (Cross 2021).

4.1.5 Penetration Strategy (Dynamic)

The *penetration strategy is* recommended for products and services with high, short-term price elasticity. It focuses on quick sales and long-term profits (Simon and Fassnacht 2016, pp. 301). Here, the new product or service is introduced at a relatively low price to create an entry barrier for competitors. Subsequently, prices can be changed, costs reduced (e.g., economies of scale), and sales increased. In the long term, there is also the possibility of achieving a strong market position through *carry-over* effects (Simon and Fassnacht 2016, pp. 301).

4.2 Innovative Pricing Models

In addition to standard pricing strategies, innovative pricing focuses on creating added value for the customer. Innovative pricing models aim to exploit individual willingness to pay optimally. The ultimate goal is to generate benefits from the customer's point of view. Table 4.1 presents a selection of exemplary, non-exhaustive pricing models and their central added value. Twelve exemplary models are described below.

4.2.1 Decoy Pricing

In *decoy* pricing, companies offer decoy prices to avoid so-called extremes and increase net margins, sometimes significantly (Mortimer 2019; Wu and Cosguner 2020). The following example illustrates: If companies offer only two products—a basic product priced at €20 and a luxury product priced at €50—the sales share will be split between these two products. Another product is now added at a higher "decoy" price. For

Table 4.1 Innovative pricing models—examples *(Source: Reinecke 2021)*

Innovative pricing models	Added value
1. Decoy pricing	Risk aversion
2. Bundling	Convenience
3. Freemium	Freedom to experiment
4. Add-on	Low base price
5. Subscription pricing	Reduced cost volatility
6. Pay-per-use/ "… as a service"	No fixed costs
7. Flat rate	Cost certainty
8. Performance-based pricing	Performance security
9. Success-based Pricing	No business risk
10. Pay-what-you-want	Satisfaction and fairness
11. Auctioning	Offset intangibles
12. Switching	Charge a third party

example, the company introduces another luxury product at €100. This "decoy price" directly influences customers' purchasing decisions. It causes more people to choose the middle product at the price of €50 than without this offer. *Decoy pricing* is particularly attractive to risk-averse customers who do not select "extreme offers" with the middle offer in place.

4.2.2 Bundling

In *bundling*, different products or services are combined into a product or service package. Some offers are exclusively offered in a bundle (pure bundle) and others in addition to single purchase (mixed bundle) (Marburger 2012). The price for the bundle is lower than the sum of the prices of all the products or services included (Armstrong and Vickers 2010; Derdenger and Kumar 2013; Michel 2014; Zhou 2017). This form of pricing is common, for example, for tableware: a tableware set is usually significantly cheaper than the sum of the individual parts. It is vital to integrate only "fast movers" or standard products into the bundle because a component whose value is not appreciated lowers the perceived value of the overall bundle. The added value for customers lies primarily in convenience: customers save costs while suppliers achieve higher volume. Furthermore, transaction costs are reduced (Nagle et al. 2011).

In *unbundling*, services are broken into individual parts to achieve a higher overall price. Unbundling is common in the airline industry, where passengers increasingly pay different prices for tickets, seats, baggage check-in, catering, and much more (Michel 2014). *Ikea* also pursues this strategy for furniture, e.g., by pricing tabletop and table legs separately.

Similar to bundling, in *tying*, the price of a service depends on the purchase of another good (Marburger 2012). Tying is common, for example, with digital offerings in the media industry, such as an eBook download on *Amazon* that can only be accessed on a *Kindle* device.

4.2.3 Freemium

Using *freemium models,* companies offer their customers subscriptions of varying scope that can be flexibly tested and booked (Gu et al. 2018; Kumar 2014). The basic version is offered free of charge, at least for a certain period. Customers enjoy the freedom to experiment with different packages and identify the right solution for them. They appreciate this flexibility. Often, the free version is financed by advertising, while a paid version is available without advertising or with higher performance (Sato 2019). *Spotify, YouTube,* and *Vimeo* offer well-known examples of freemium models.

4.2.4 Add-on

With *add-on pricing,* customers pay a low base price and, at will, add additional products or services (*add-ons*) for additional costs (Ellison 2005; Marburger 2012; Schüwer and Kosfeld 2010). Typical examples are memberships (basic fee with the option to book additional services) and vehicle equipment in the automotive industry. It is also possible to purchase additional options or packages from mobile communications companies to supplement one's subscription.

4.2.5 Subscription

In *subscription models*, customers pay a regular recurring fee for a product, service, or membership (Kübler et al. 2021). They benefit from cost certainty and convenience. Subscriptions are fixed-fee subscriptions per service period, such as online news, gym subscriptions, *Spotify,* and *iCloud* (Chyi 2005; Danaher 2002). They are widespread in services but increasingly found in consumer goods. At *Blacksocks.com* in Switzerland, it has been possible for many years to subscribe to three pairs of socks three times a year in a standard subscription. *Amazon* also offers so-called savings subscriptions.

4.2.6 Pay-per-Use

With *pay-per-use*, no fixed costs are incurred. Instead, prices are charged based on the actual service provided (Balasubramanian et al. 2015; Skiera and Lambrecht 2006). A typical example is copying costs per page at *Xerox*. This approach is particularly suitable for capital goods or expensive consumer durables because it does not require initial investment and makes costs more flexible. Similarly, at *Gillette*, in addition to fixed costs for the razor, costs occur for razor blades depending on actual use (Michel 2014).

4.2.7 Flat Rate

Flat rates are a kind of "ultra bundle" (Michel 2014)—a variety of bundled services—at a fixed price. The key added value for customers is cost certainty and convenience (Michel 2014; Skiera and Lambrecht 2006). A typical example is all-inclusive fares on cruise ships or club vacations (Michel 2014). Instead of paying individual prices for flight, hotel, food, beverages, sports, and leisure activities, a flat rate offers a total package with a guaranteed price. The total price for the vacation is already known at the time of booking. It includes all ancillary and variable services such as food and beverages.

These offers are increasingly gaining acceptance among mobile communications companies because, from the customer's point of view, price intransparency is replaced by security.

4.2.8 Performance-Based Pricing

In *performance-based pricing*, the focus is on performance security or guarantee (Shapiro 2002). Customers only pay the provider when specific targets are achieved, as in a management-by-objectives system. For example, payments are often linked to certain service levels in the information technology industry, such as server availability, click rates, or response times (Hu et al. 2012).

4.2.9 Success-Based Pricing

Success-based or *outcome-based pricing* is a maximum version of performance-based pricing (Adida 2021). Here, customers do not assume any risk: The price is only due if, for example, a service leads to success (Shapiro 2002). An example of this is so-called contingency fees, common among US attorneys: the plaintiff only incurs attorney's fees if a lawsuit for damages is successful. The attorney's fee is often calculated as a percentage of the damages obtained, not according to time and effort (e.g., working hours).

4.2.10 Pay-What-You-Want

Pay-what-you-want is a participatory price management method (Kim et al. 2009). The focus is on customer satisfaction and fairness. The added value for customers is that they decide about the value of a product or service (Kim et al. 2009; Michel 2014; Schmidt et al. 2015).

In contrast to public auctions, the individual willingness to pay in pay-what-you-want is invisible to other co-bidders (Michel 2014). The Ibis hotel chain provides an example with the *Ibis test week*. Customers did not have to pay a pre-agreed price for their overnight stay during a promotional week but could decide how much the stay was worth upon departure. In this way, the company wanted to convince customers of its value—and at the same time, tested its price–performance ratio in a field experiment. In 2007, the English rock band *Radiohead* also offered to download their album for a freely selectable amount, surpassing any previous download revenue (Kim et al. 2009).

Applying the *pay-what-you-want strategy* can be dangerous if willingness to pay is uncertain. Therefore, good customer knowledge and segmentation are essential: At a French luxury restaurant and for gourmands and business customers, the pricing model may be successful, while too many *McDonald's* customers may take advantage of the offer and pay nothing.

4.2.11 Auctioning

Auctioning allows companies to charge for intangible values and maximize individual willingness to pay (Zeithammer and Liu 2006). For example, *Google* promises the greatest advertising visibility to the highest bidders (Michel 2014). Auctions are discussed in detail in *Chap. 6*.

4.2.12 Switching

Switching is a strategic method of innovative price management. A third party—not the end customer—assumes the costs (Michel 2014). Traditionally, this is the case with newspaper publishers. The reader only pays a (small) part of the product cost or nothing in the case of free papers. In return, the advertisers bear the costs. One example is *20 Minuten*: the Swiss newspaper is distributed free of charge to 2 million readers on public transport and financed by high advertising costs (Michel 2014).

Another example is the Swiss company *Lifestraw*, which offers water filters against bacteria and parasites (Michel 2014). The need for these products is particularly great among poorer customers in rural areas in Africa, but financial resources are lacking. The water filters are (partially) financed through CO_2 credits through switching. The energy savings for boiling water can compensate for unecological behavior such as air travel (see *carbonfootprint.com*).

4.3 Price Differentiation and Variation

Price differentiation and variation are essential instruments of active price management. In this context, price differences are not due to cost differences but are based on differences in customers' willingness to pay (Marburger 2012, p. 45; Seufert 2014). If a unit price is perceived as "too expensive," the sales volume and thus the contribution margin decrease. If a unit price is too low, the sales volume increases, but the customers' willingness to pay is not optimally exploited. Three prerequisites for successful price differentiation are that (1) the company is a "price maker," i.e., has market power in a monopolistic or oligopolistic market, (2) customers can be divided into different customer segments with different levels of willingness to pay, and (3) these customer segments are separate from each other ('fencing') (Seufert 2014). In the case of price differentiation and variation, companies strive to skim off different levels of existing willingness to pay through segmentation (Diller et al. 2021, pp. 363; Simon and Fassnacht 2016, pp. 233). As a result, higher and lower prices can generate additional contribution margins and revenue. Thus, *quantitative price targets* are optimized (see Fig. 4.2). Whereas with a uniform price, some customers do not buy because it is too expensive, and others would be willing to pay more, differentiated prices increase contribution margins (= green area in Fig. 4.2). Here, it was assumed that the proportional costs are zero (as is the case, e.g., with some software licenses). A prerequisite for this strategy is that customer segments can be separated ("fencing").

On the other hand, there is a risk that differentiation and variation have a negative impact on *qualitative price targets*. For example, differentiated and variable prices can affect price confidence and price satisfaction, leading to price confusion (Michel and Pfäffli 2013). In addition, price differentiation and variation increase complexity in price management, so pricing strategies must be carefully planned, implemented, and communicated.

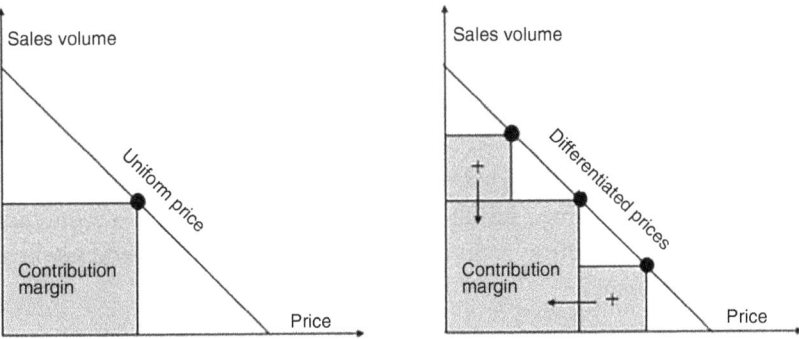

Fig. 4.2 Additional contribution margin through price differentiation (assuming proportional costs of 0) *(Source: Own illustration)*

4.3.1 Comparison of Price Differentiation Strategies

A distinction is made between *criteria-based* price differentiation (person-related, spatial, temporal) and *self-selection* (service-related, bundling, nonlinear pricing, multi-person pricing) (Fassnacht 2003). If prices are actively varied by the company—depending on pre-defined criteria—this is called *criteria-based* price differentiation (e.g., *Deutsche Bahn AG* savings prices). In this case, customers have only one option to choose from at any given time. If customers can choose between different price-performance combinations at a given point—depending on individual preference and willingness to pay—this is called *self-selection* (e.g., business vs. economy class; Simon and Fassnacht 2016, pp. 246). Table 4.2 visualizes the possible strategies.

The following subtypes are distinguished (Fassnacht 2003, pp. 483):

1. Price differentiation linked to criteria:

    (a) *Person-based price differentiation*
    (b) *Spatial price differentiation*
    (c) *Price differentiation over time*

2. Self-selection:

    (a) *Performance-based price differentiation*
    (b) *Bundling*
    (c) *Nonlinear pricing, multi-person pricing*

4.3.2 Criteria-Based Price Differentiation

In *criteria-based price differentiation*, similar products or services are offered at different prices. Differentiation is based on standard segmentation models. A distinction is made between *personal, spatial,* and *temporal price differentiation*.

(a) *Personal price differentiation*

If customer segments differ in their willingness or ability to pay, prices can be differentiated on a *person-by-person basis*. For example, students

Table 4.2 Differentiation strategies (Source: Own presentation based on Fassnacht 2003, pp. 483)

Differentiation strategies					
Bound by criteria			"Self-selection"		
(a) Person-related price differentiation	(b) Spatial price differentiation	(c) Time-based price differentiation	(a) Service-related price differentiation	(b) Bundling	(c) Nonlinear pricing, multi-person pricing.

and trainees can be granted discounts, or employees can be allowed to purchase their own company's offerings at preferential conditions.

The forms of differentiation can be personal, regional, temporal, or based on the design of other marketing instruments, such as distribution. Implementation problems exist in the definition and separation of segments (Simon and Fassnacht 2016, pp. 235): *fencing* (e.g., Zhang and Bell 2012) ensures that segments can be separated, for example, by requiring students to show their student card if they want to receive a discount.

(b) *Spatial price differentiation*

In *spatial price differentiation,* prices are varied depending on location (e.g., location, region, and country) (Zhang 2012). One example is *McDonald's* spatial price differentiation: in 2020, a Big Mac cost US$6.71 in Switzerland, $4.41 in England, and $2.15 in South Africa (Burgernomics 2021).

International pricing is a particular case of regional price differentiation. International price differences have different internal and external causes. Internal causes are, for example, the entrepreneurial performance of the previous period, company forecasts and strategic targets, specific costs, distribution structure, market performance design, and company organization. External causes are different legal framework conditions, customs duties and levies, macroeconomic factors such as economic growth and inflation, market and competitive structure, region-specific customer preferences, and customer behavior.

> **Excursus—*International price differentiation vs. harmonization***
>
> Excessive international price differentials can be problematic because they tempt market participants to engage in arbitrage and are perceived as politically critical. Differentiated prices better achieve quantitative price targets, but price differentiation also creates complexity costs. Therefore, it may make sense to reduce the price differentials: prices that are too high should be lowered, or parallel imports should be accepted; prices that are too low should be increased, or the company's offerings should no longer be offered to prevent arbitrage. In the resulting *international price corridor* (see Fig. 4.3), optimal contribution margins are generated, and parallel imports are reduced (based on Simon 1992).

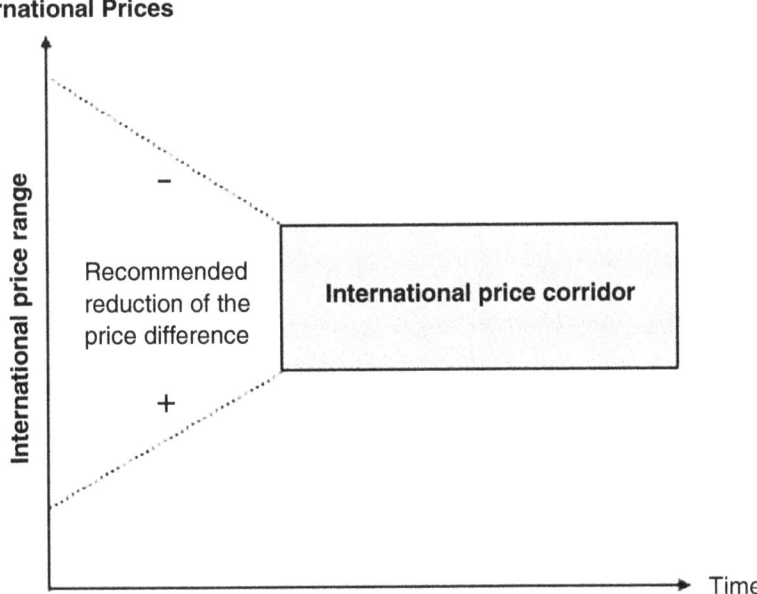

Fig. 4.3 International price corridor *(Source: Own illustration based on Simon 1992)*

International price management measures are challenging for companies because price harmonization deprives countries of a main design parameter, the price. Consequently, these companies are no longer entirely responsible for their regional economic result.

The following ten theses support companies in dealing with international price harmonization or differentiation (based on Belz and Mühlmeier 2000):

1. *Get international price transparency!*
   Do this before your most important customers do.

2. *Analyze the causes of price differences in different countries.*
   Also, assess your customers' tendency to obtain and compare international price information.

3. *Compare the advantages and disadvantages of active price harmonization with the chances of a reactive approach, i.e., maintaining price differences.*
4. *Evaluate opportunities for differentiation in marketing.*
   Does differentiation in marketing allow you to take a local approach in different countries?

5. *Select those customers and services for which price harmonization seems urgent.*
6. *Develop dynamic solutions if harmonization is necessary.*
   To do so, determine the international price corridor.

7. *Determine solutions for global and regional pricing systems simultaneously.*
   For example, enforce local price differentials and offer compensation or bonuses for key accounts.

8. *Negotiate with key accounts for price harmonization offsets.*
   Such quid pro quos may include major purchasing decisions, a joint development strategy, or a joint international growth strategy.

9. *Combine price harmonization with international service packages for customers (e.g., bundling).*
10. *Review the (de)centralized management and the commissions of your international subsidiaries.*

(c) *Time-based price differentiation*

Price differentiation over time is called *price variation* (Fassnacht 2003, p. 13). It involves varying discounts or surcharges for identical products depending on calendar time, daytime, or time of order (Fassnacht 2003, p. 494). Examples include *introductory offers, money-saving tickets, seasonal discounts,* and *daily* or *special offers.* Price variation only makes sense if there is demand for a particular product or service at different times. A distinction is made between "peak" and "off-peak" times (Marburger 2012). In addition, price variation must be carefully planned to prevent negative effects such as image damage, "hoarding purchases," a permanently low willingness to pay, or a peak reversal. Peak reversal occurs, for example, if numerous customers would postpone their movie visit to a discounted movie day so that discounted admissions would replace regular visits. Peak reversal does not happen on typical cinema days such as Mondays because many people are inflexible in their demand and only visit the cinema on weekends. Price variation is common, especially in the transportation and tourism industries. For example, airline or hotel prices rise with shorter lead times and increasing demand.

> **Price variation—*Example: Deutsche Bahn AG***
>
> Deutsche Bahn AG calculates its prices according to the length of the journey and rewards long-term planning with "Savings Prices." These are available in fixed quotas up to 3 days before departure and feature discounts of 25–50%. The *Swiss Federal Railways* even offer savings tickets at discounts of up to 70%. Short-term bookings are made at the higher but flexible "normal price."

One challenge of time-based price differentiation is capacity utilization: When, as in this case, time-based price differentiation is combined with volume-based quotas to achieve optimal capacity utilization, this is referred to as *"yield management"* or *"average yield management"* (Donaghy et al. 1995). In yield management, the highest possible prices are realized at each time. This is possible when different customer groups have different demand curves. A typical example is the seat load factor at airlines (Vinod 2021).

4.3.3 Self-Selection

With *self-selection,* different prices are set for similar but differentiated products or services. Customers choose the most suitable price–performance combination depending on their own needs. Price decisions are based on individual preferences and willingness to pay (Marburger 2012).

(a) *Performance-related price differentiation*

In *performance-based price differentiation*, prices are differentiated based on product characteristics, like quality and time. The aim is to maximize customer-specific willingness to pay and create incentives for cross-selling and upselling. For this purpose, companies create different product or service versions from which customers can choose. For example, airlines differentiate between business and economy fares in terms of comfort, catering, flexibility, baggage allowance, and check-in speed.

(b) *Price bundling*

Price bundling is of interest to multi-product companies. Here, individual products are combined into a bundle and offered at a lower price than the sum of the individual prices. The bundle taps into customers' existing willingness to pay and induces additional consumption. For example, the computer manufacturer *Dell* offers bundles consisting of a PC, monitor, software, peripherals, and service that are significantly cheaper than the sum of the individual parts.

> **Price bundling—*example: McDonald's***
>
> *McDonald's* takes advantage of its customers' additional willingness to pay to buy another drink, side dish, or meal for a small additional amount with its successful menus. In addition, *McDonald's* offers larger portions with the so-called Menu plus. In this way, the company triggers additional consumption because the customers' willingness to pay for the remainder is skimmed off. From a financial perspective, this strategy is very successful. It is controversial regarding customer protection because it tempts them to eat more than they had initially planned.

(c) *Nonlinear pricing, multi-person pricing.*

Nonlinear pricing is recommended when the price determines the consumed quantity of units (Tacke 2013). Here, the focus is on customer loyalty and increasing revenue. The price is varied depending on the consumption, size, performance, and attractiveness of the customer. The basic price can decrease *continuously* (4 for €10, 5 for €12, 6 for €13.50) or *discontinuously* (4 for €10, 8 for €15, 16 for €20) as the quantity increases. Nonlinear pricing is common practice in the sale of photographs, for example, passport photos. It incentivizes increased consumption, leads to customer loyalty, skims of willingness to pay, and increases revenues.

Further examples can be found in the communications, electricity, and public transport sectors: *Two-part tariffs* consisting of a basic charge and a usage fee are common in telecommunications. There are so-called *block tariffs* in the electricity and water industries where the price increases after a certain level of consumption; customers can often choose different models. In the rail transport sector, the BahnCard from *Deutsche Bahn AG* or the Halbtax from *Swiss Federal Railways* offers a *two-part tariff* consisting of a basic fee (the subscription price) and a lower fare per route. Customers themselves must assess whether a subscription is worthwhile because they regularly travel. The basic fee is particularly attractive for providers because it is incurred in advance, regardless of service usage, and can be used to cover investments or fixed costs. Figure 4.4 illustrates that the combination of fixed and proportional prices optimally skims off willingness to pay. Without a basic charge, the transport price for the train could be €0.30 per kilometer. With a basic charge, the charge could be €75 for a BahnCard 50, leading to a choice between €0.40 per kilometer (without BahnCard) and €0.20 per kilometer (with BahnCard).

A particular case of price differentiation is *multi-person pricing* (Simon and Fassnacht 2016, p. 257): Examples are group, family, or streaming prices that depend on the number of persons, for example, in leisure, entertainment, and tourism.

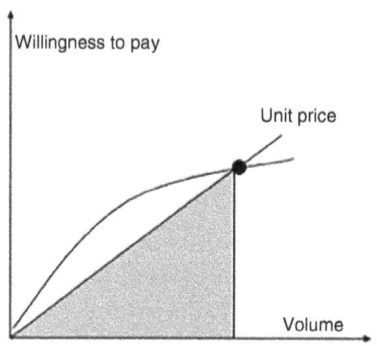 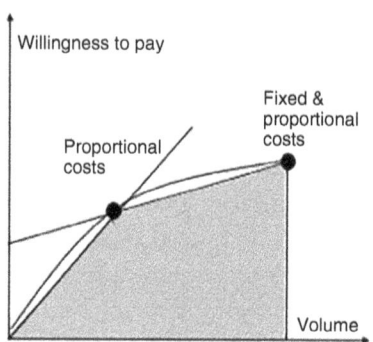

Fig. 4.4 Higher absorption of willingness to pay through nonlinear pricing (Source: Own illustration)

References

Adida, E. (2021). Outcome-based pricing for new pharmaceuticals via rebates. *Management Science, 67*(2), 892–913.
Armstrong, M., & Vickers, J. (2010). Competitive non-linear pricing and bundling. *The Review of Economic Studies, 77*(1), 30–60.
Balasubramanian, S., Bhattacharya, S., & Krishnan, V. V. (2015). Pricing information goods: A strategic analysis of the selling and pay-per-use mechanisms. *Marketing Science, 34*(2), 218–234.
Belz, C., & Mühlmeier, J. (2000). *International price management [International pricing]: Strategy, price harmonization, tools, case studies*. Ueberrether.
Burgernomics: The Big Mac index. (2021, July 21). *The Economist*. https://www.economist.com/big-mac-index
Chyi, H. I. (2005). Willingness to pay for online news: An empirical study on the viability of the subscription model. *Journal of Media Economics, 18*(2), 131–142.
Cross, J. (2021, September 14). iPhone 12: Buy now or wait? *Macworld*. https://www.macworld.com/article/352162/iphone-12-pro-buy-or-wait-specs-price.html
Danaher, P. J. (2002). Optimal pricing of new subscription services: Analysis of a market experiment. *Marketing Science, 21*(2), 119–138.
Derdenger, T., & Kumar, V. (2013). The dynamic effects of bundling as a product strategy. *Marketing Science, 32*(6), 827–859.

Diller, H., Beinert, M., Ivens, B., & Müller, S. (2021). *Pricing: Prinzipien und Prozesse der betrieblichen Preispolitik* (5th ed.). Kohlhammer.

Donaghy, K., McMahon, U., & McDowell, D. (1995). Yield management: An overview. *International Journal of Hospitality Management, 14*(2), 139–150.

Ellison, G. (2005). A model of add-on pricing. *The Quarterly Journal of Economics, 120*(2), 585–637.

Fassnacht, M. (2003). Preisdifferenzierung. In *Handbuch Preispolitik* (pp. 483–502). Gabler.

Froböse, M. (2016). Strategische Marketing-Planung. In *Marketing* (pp. 59–88). Springer Gabler.

Gu, X., Kannan, P. K., & Ma, L. (2018). Selling the premium in freemium. *Journal of Marketing, 82*(6), 10–27.

Hu, Y., Shin, J., & Tang, Z. (2012). *Performance-based pricing models in online advertising: Cost per click versus cost per action.* Georgia Institute.

Kim, J. Y., Natter, M., & Spann, M. (2009). Pay what you want: A new participative pricing mechanism. *Journal of Marketing, 73*(1), 44–58.

Kübler, R., Seifert, R., & Kandziora, M. (2021). Content valuation strategies for digital subscription platforms. *Journal of Cultural Economics, 45*, 295–326.

Kucher, E. (1985). Preisresponsedynamik: Theorie und Messung. In *Scannerdaten und Preissensitivität bei Konsumgütern* (pp. 88–206). Gabler.

Kumar, V. (2014). Making "freemium" work. *Harvard Business Review, 92*(5), 27–29.

Marburger, D. (2012). *Innovative pricing strategies to increase profits.* Business Expert Press.

Michel, S. (2014). Capture more value. *Harvard Business Review, 92*(10), 20.

Michel, S., & Pfäffli, P. (2013). Obstacles to implementing value-based pricing. *Perspectives for Managers, 185*, 1–4.

Mortimer, G. (2019). The decoy effect: How you are influenced to choose without really knowing it. *The Conversation*, 1–6.

Nagle, T. T., Hogan, J., & Zale, J. (2011). *The strategy and tactics of pricing: A guide to growing more profitably.* Prentice Hall.

Reinecke, S. (1996). Management von IT-Outsourcing-Kooperationen: *Marketing für komplexe Informationstechnologie-Dienstleistungen.* Dissertation, University of St. Gallen.

Reinecke, S. (2021): Price Management. Lecture Slides University of St. Gallen. St. Gallen

Sato, S. (2019). Freemium as optimal menu pricing. *International Journal of Industrial Organization, 63*, 480–510

Schmidt, K. M., Spann, M., & Zeithammer, R. (2015). Pay what you want as a marketing strategy in monopolistic and competitive markets. *Management Science, 61*(6), 1217–1236.

Schüwer, U., & Kosfeld, M. (2010). *Add-on pricing, consumer myopia and regulatory intervention*. ZBW.

Seufert, E. B. (2014). *Freemium economics: Leveraging analytics and user segmentation to drive revenue*. Elsevier.

Shapiro, B. P. (2002, July 22). *Is performance-based pricing the right price for you?*. Harvard Business School. https://hbswk.hbs.edu/item/is-performance-based-pricing-the-right-price-for-you

Shapiro, B. P. (2003, February 10). *Commodity busters: Be a price maker, not a price taker*. Harvard Business School. https://hbswk.hbs.edu/item/commodity-busters-be-a-price-maker-not-a-price-taker

Siems, F. (2009). *Preismanagement: Konzepte – Strategien – Instrumente*. Vahlens Handbücher.

Simon, H. (1979). Dynamische Erklärungen des Nachfragerverhaltens aus Carryover-Effekt und Responsefunktion. In *Consumer Behavior and Information* (pp. 415–444). Gabler.

Simon, H. (1992). *Price management: Analysis-strategy-implementation* (2nd ed.). Springer.

Simon, H., & Fassnacht, M. (2016). *Preismanagement: Strategie – Analyse – Entscheidung – Umsetzung* (4th ed.). Springer.

Skiera, B., & Lambrecht, A. (2006). Flat rate versus pay-per-use pricing. In *Turbulence in the telecommunications and media industry* (pp. 77–101). Springer.

Steinert-Threlkeld, T. (1993): Pricing approach sets company apart, in: The Dallas Morning News, "EDS: The Next Horizon.", Dallas, Texas, pp. 44–45.

Tacke, G. (2013). *Nichtlineare Preisbildung: Höhere Gewinne durch Differenzierung* (Vol. 64). Springer.

Vinod, B. (2021). *The evolution of yield management in the airline industry*. Springer.

Wu, C., & Cosguner, K. (2020). Profiting from the decoy effect: A case study of an online diamond retailer. *Marketing Science, 39*(5), 974–995.

Zeithammer, R., & Liu, P. (2006). *When is auctioning preferred to posting a fixed selling price?* University of Chicago.

Zhang, B. (2012). Capacity-constrained multiple-market price discrimination. *Computers & Operations Research, 39*(1), 105–111.

Zhang, M., & Bell, P. (2012). Price fencing in the practice of revenue management: An overview and taxonomy. *Journal of Revenue and Pricing Management, 11*(2), 146–159.

Zhou, J. (2017). Competitive bundling. *Econometrica, 85*(1), 145–172.

5

Price Management for Innovations

When companies launch innovations, they are confronted with different challenges: They may not yet have a clear idea of the target audience and the target application or function of the new offering. The go-to-market strategy may not yet be defined, and marketing and sales personnel may not yet be in place. Most importantly, a pricing model may not have been established, and the price-sales function for the company's innovative offering may be unknown. Then, it is essential to estimate the perceived value of the innovation from the customer's perspective.

The perceived customer value can be determined by observation, questioning, or mixed forms. These include *real market data, price experiments, lotteries and auctions,* and *customer* or *expert surveys* (Simon and Fassnacht 2016, pp. 123; Völckner 2006).

As part of *real market data,* prices of similar products, other countries, or pilot markets can be consulted. *Price experiments* can be conducted as laboratory or field experiments. For example, one can vary the price in comparable stores or sales regions to capture the willingness to pay. *Lotteries and auctions* can determine (maximum) individual willingness to pay. *Experts* can also help with the assessment and price management of innovations. Attempts are often made to determine willingness to pay through customer surveys. *Direct questioning* may jeopardize the validity of the results, e.g., because people cannot assess their willingness to pay or are dishonest. For this reason, *indirect* price surveys do not focus on price as the sole variable.

Depending on the offering's degree of innovation (from low to high), the following price-setting options are common:

1. *Observation:* Market data
2. *Survey:* Customer survey
    (a) *Direct (Gabor–Granger method or Van Westendorp analysis)*
    (b) *Indirect (Conjoint analysis)*

3. *Mixed form*: Price experiments
4. *Survey:* Expert survey (Delphi method)

5.1 Use of Available Market Data

To set an appropriate price for innovations with *(1) a low degree of innovation*, companies can draw on available market data of similar products. For example, if a new *Milka* chocolate is introduced, the price can be based on the prices of previous chocolates.

5.2 Customer Survey

To set an appropriate price for innovations with *(2) a low to medium degree of innovation*, companies can determine their customers' willingness to pay by conducting direct or indirect customer surveys.

5.2.1 Direct Customer Survey

The *Gabor–Granger method* or the *Van Westendorp analysis* are often used for direct customer surveys.

(a) **Gabor–Granger method**

The *Gabor–Granger method* determines the optimal price based on the price-sales function. It is named after André *Gabor* and Clive *Granger* in 1964 and is considered a standard method for determining willingness to pay using *direct customer surveys* (Gabor and Granger 1964). The method intends to determine the *optimal price* for a product or service by querying the purchase probability for a service X as a function of the price Y. The price of the offering is determined by the customer's willingness to pay. To determine the price-sales function, customers are asked several questions about the probability of purchase at different prices (Gabor and Granger 1964), for example:

Gabor–Granger method—*purchase probability questions*

How likely is it that you will receive service X for …
1. … CHF 125 buy?
2. … CHF 100 buy?
3. … CHF 75 buy?

Respondents choose between each of the following answers:
1. Very likely
2. More likely
3. Draw
4. Rather unlikely
5. Very unlikely

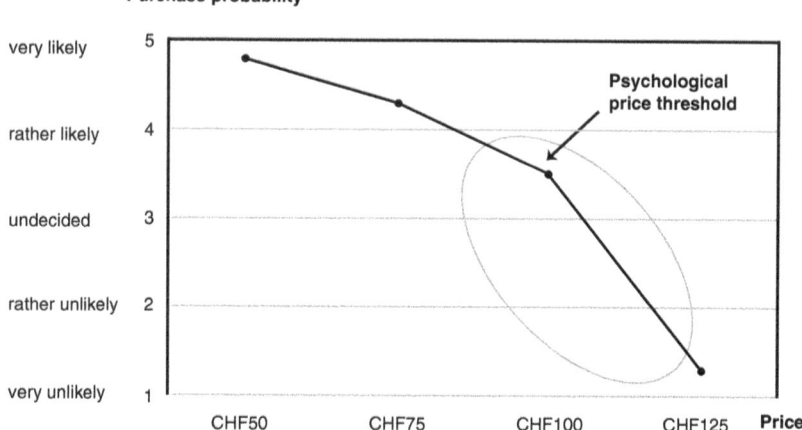

Fig. 5.1 Gabor–Granger method: aggregated purchase probabilities *(Source: Own illustration adapted from* Gabor and Granger 1964*)*

By aggregating the purchase probabilities, a *psychological price threshold* can be identified. This price threshold is the price at which the purchase probability changes from *undecided* to *more likely*. Figure 5.1 visualizes the aggregated purchase probabilities.

The *Gabor–Granger method* has various advantages: It provides information on the perceived value of an offering and the individual willingness to pay (Lipovetsky et al. 2011, pp. 168; Völckner 2006, p. 35). Likewise, it enables companies to identify price thresholds. The method is inexpensive, simple to perform, and easy to visualize. It is particularly recommended if companies already have a rough idea of the price (Lipovetsky et al. 2011, p. 170).

However, the method also has disadvantages: First, it does not consider the competitive situation. Second, it does not provide exact price elasticities and thus does not offer any simulation options, for example, for determining a profit-optimized price. Third, this method places an artificial focus on price due to the direct survey. This can lead to an overemphasis of the price or consumers being overcharged because they have not yet formed an opinion (Lipovetsky et al. 2011, p. 170).

(b) *Van Westendorp analysis*

Van Westendorp analysis is a *direct customer survey* method. It became known in 1976 after the Dutch economist *van Westendorp* and is considered a standard method for determining willingness to pay (Reinecke et al. 2009; Sullivan 2003). The idea is that there is an *acceptable price range* for each product or service and that customers do not buy if prices are too high (insufficient price–performance ratio) or too low (presumed low product quality) (Diller 2008, p. 404). To determine willingness to pay, customers are first asked four questions about their price thresholds (Van Westendorp 1976):

> **Van Westendorp Analysis—*Four Key Questions***
>
> At what price would you estimate the product ...
> 1. ... as cheap/as a really good deal?
> 2. ... as expensive, but at least worth considering?
> 3. ... as too cheap, so the quality is questionable?
> 4. ... as too expensive, so you would not buy it (again)?

Subsequently, customers' responses are aggregated and presented in a diagram (Wildner 2003, p. 6): on the abscissa the price and on the ordinate the cumulative proportion of respondents. The *optimum price* can be read from the intersection of the "too expensive" and "too cheap" curves. This point indicates the price at which the resistance to purchase is lowest or the interest in purchasing is greatest. Here, customers are most likely to buy the product because it is neither too cheap nor too expensive (Lewis and Shoemaker 1997, p. 48). Another relevant point is the *indifference point*. This point reflects either the average market price or the price of the market leader.

Figure 5.2 visualizes the *Van Westendorp analysis* and illustrates the *optimal price point* and the *indifference point*.

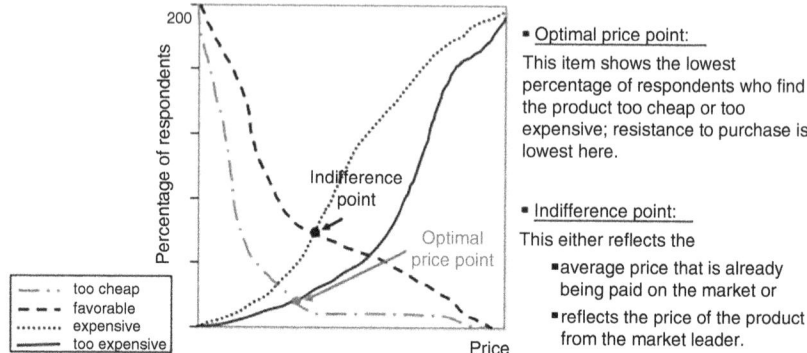

Fig. 5.2 Van Westendorp analysis: determining the optimum price *(Source: Reinecke et al. 2009, p. 99)*

Furthermore, the Van Westendorp analysis provides information on the *acceptable price range* or the *limits of acceptable prices*: The upper and lower limits are formed by the intersections of the curves "too expensive" and "not expensive" and "too cheap" and "not cheap." Outside this price range, products are perceived as too expensive or too cheap. In other words, purchase interest is too low, or purchase resistance is too high (Lewis and Shoemaker 1997, p. 48). The smaller the acceptable price range, the greater customers' price sensitivity. Figure 5.3 illustrates the *acceptable price range*.

The *Van Westendorp analysis* has several advantages and disadvantages (Reinecke et al. 2009): It is suitable to estimate prices for innovative products for which no asking price exists yet, or for products for which no competitive environment exists. However, it is crucial that customers can imagine the innovative potential. Above all, the method helps to determine the *acceptable price range*. Depending on their mindset, price managers will lean toward maximum price or minimum purchase resistance within this range. Also, simple visualization is an advantage. In short, the *Van Westendorp analysis* is a simple, inexpensive, and efficient method for determining willingness to pay (Lyon 2002, p. 10).

Despite its frequent mention, the method is often criticized in theory (e.g., Breidert et al. 2006). Its validity is disputed because it does not consider competitive situations and does not provide strict price

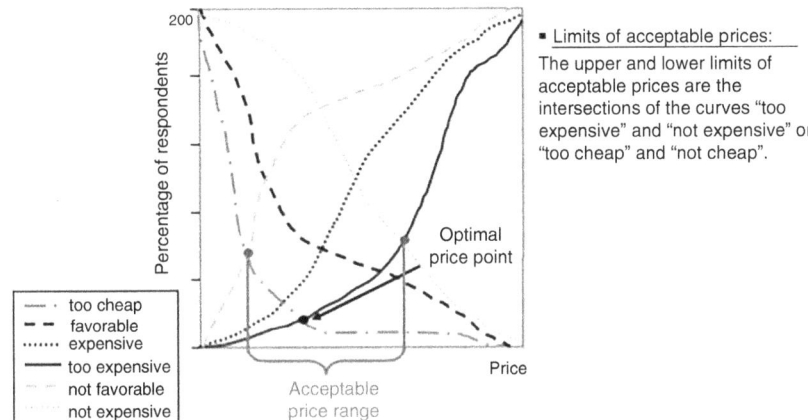

Fig. 5.3 Determining the acceptable price range *(Source:* Reinecke et al. 2009, p. 98)

elasticities or simulation possibilities (Diller et al. 2021, pp. 189). Moreover, it can lead to an overemphasis on price (Reinecke et al. 2009).

5.2.2 Indirect Customer Survey: Conjoint Analysis

Conjoint analysis is an *indirect customer survey* method. The underlying idea is that offerings can be broken down into characteristics. Therefore, customers are *not* asked directly about the price or the properties of a product or service but weigh up between realistic offers. By systematically varying prices and characteristics, utility values are determined. These are decisive for determining an appropriate price.

The advantages of *conjoint analysis* lie in precisely determining customer wishes and individual values. The method does not focus on price but customer values. Since no direct questions are asked about the price or the characteristics of market service, and if carried out correctly, the results are of high validity.

The disadvantages of *conjoint analysis* are that it is very time-consuming and costly, and that precise knowledge of the product and service characteristics is required: the characteristics relevant to purchasing must be known. Only then can the right criteria be selected for the survey.

Otherwise, the method risks an overly subjective selection of seemingly relevant characteristics *("trash in—trash out")*. In addition, the selected criteria must be of similar relevance. Otherwise, one criterion (e.g., design) could be highly relevant for the purchase decision and outshine the others.

The *conjoint analysis* is divided into five steps (Backhaus et al. 2021, pp. 577).

1. Selection of properties and property characteristics
2. Creation of the survey design
3. Stimuli evaluation
4. Estimation of the utility function
5. Interpretation of the part-worth values

First, the properties and characteristics are determined through expert interviews, desk research, or brainstorming. All properties should be relevant for management and vary in practice. They should be clearly defined and communicable and should not have strong correlations. Moreover, the characteristics should influence preferences. Then, the survey design is determined together with experts. For this purpose, the combinations of characteristics (stimuli) presented to the customers for evaluation are determined. The characteristics should be unambiguous, realistic, unbiased, sufficiently separated from each other, and interesting for management. Subsequently, the stimuli are evaluated. A distinction is made between *(a) ranking-based, (b) rating-based,* and *(c) choice-based evaluation.* The resulting values are used to define partial utility values and, finally, utility values for all properties and characteristics.

(a) *Ranking-based rating*

In *ranking-based conjoint analysis,* customers are asked to assign a ranking value to each service package. The ranking values reflect the customers' preference for the respective packages (e.g., 1 = 1st preference, 5th last preference). The smaller the rank value, the greater the preference for the package.

(b) *Rating-based*

In *ranking-based conjoint analysis,* customers are asked to rate each service package on a scale (e.g., 1 = least preferred; 10 = most preferred). Each position on the scale can only be assigned once. The rating reflects the preference for the respective packages. The better the rating, the greater the preference for the package.

(c) *Choice-based*

In *choice-based conjoint analysis,* customers are asked to select the service package they consider most attractive from a range of service packages or rate different service packages on a scale (e.g., 0–5 stars). Each item on the scale can be mentioned more than once. The summary rating reflects the preferences for the respective packages. The better the rating, the stronger the preference. Overall, there should be few (<6) properties and (<6) expressions per property, and a balanced number of expressions between properties, as well as realistic levels between expressions. The importance of individual properties is thus not artificially emphasized so that estimation errors are reduced, and measurement scale effects are avoided.

In addition to the above forms, there are other forms of *conjoint analysis* (Eggers and Sattler 2011), e.g.:

- *Adaptive conjoint analysis:* Only the critical properties identified in a previous evaluation are available for selection.
- *Hierarchically individualized limit conjoint analysis:* The five most important attributes according to customers are adopted in the *rating-based conjoint analysis*. A "limit map" separates the attractive options from those which respondents would not choose.
- *Adaptive choice-based conjoint analysis*: Before the actual analysis, the relevant properties are defined through a consideration set ("build-your-own optimal product").

5.3 Price Experiments

Price experiments can be conducted either through laboratory or market tests (Kuss et al. 2018, pp. 217): Market tests offer the same service—for a short period and under controlled conditions at different prices in different test markets. Different test markets are considered, for example, through *store tests* (different stores), *regional test markets* (different locations/regions), or electronic *micro-test markets* (data collection for a household panel, e.g., *GfK* "BehaviorScan"). Price experiments are particularly suitable for offerings with low to medium innovation content. An example of a realistic price experiment would be new vegan products at different prices in different stores.

5.4 Expert Survey/Delphi Method

Another method for determining the price of innovative offerings is the *Delphi method* or *Delphi technique* (Powell 2003). It is an established method of *sequential expert questioning* in which multiple rounds of interviews are conducted with experts. Multi-round interviewing strives to establish consensus regarding a topic of inquiry (Powell 2003, p. 376). It is particularly suitable when end customers cannot assess the benefits of an offering because it is too innovative. An extreme example is the "beaming" of objects from one place to another.

The actual survey proceeds as follows (Powell 2003; Rowe et al. 1991): In the first round of questioning, an open-ended and unstructured qualitative survey is conducted to solicit an extensive range of response options. In this process, respondents are asked about an optimal price for the product or service. They are also asked to justify their assessment in detail. Subsequently, the qualitative data are evaluated and summarized, for example, through content analysis (Powell 2003, pp. 378). All individual expert assessments are made available to the other interviewees. Respondents are then asked whether they would like to adjust their evaluation based on the other experts' opinions. This procedure is repeated

2–3 times. The aggregated answers in the last round of questions reflect the consensus of the experts. They form the recommended price corridor.

The *Delphi method is* based on the fundamental assumption that the combined knowledge of several experts is better than the knowledge of a single expert (Rowe et al. 1991, pp. 236). The method is established in business and health care (Powell 2003, pp. 376): Its success depends on the number and qualifications of experts and their (ideally heterogeneous) composition. Ideally, experts have a diverse professional background to cover many perspectives.

A practical field of application is the price determination for a new *Apple Macintosh* device. For this purpose, the expert group could consist of an *ETH* computer science professor, the head of *Apple*'s customer club, a category manager from *Digitec Galaxus*, the editor-in-chief of *Kassensturz*, a price management researcher, and an IT market specialist.

Overall, the method is considered fast and effective. It is particularly suitable for unexplored fields. Accordingly, it is recommended, especially when data are lacking or inadequate, to describe the object of study (Rowe et al. 1991, p. 236).

One disadvantage of the *Delphi method* is that there are no uniform implementation guidelines. The method's success depends mainly on the rigor of its implementation (Powell 2003, p. 380). In addition, duration and cost vary depending on the questionnaire, the number of rounds, and the incentivization of the experts (Powell 2003, p. 377).

References

Backhaus, K., Erichson, B., Gensler, S., Weiber, R., & Weiber, T. (2021). Conjoint-analyse. In *Multivariate Analysemethoden* (pp. 577–653). Springer Gabler.

Breidert, C., Hahsler, M., & Reutterer, T. (2006). A review of methods for measuring willingness-to-pay. *Innovative Marketing, 2*(4), 8–32.

Diller, H. (2008). Price fairness. *Journal of Product & Brand Management, 17*(5), 353–355.

Diller, H., Beinert, M., Ivens, B., & Müller, S. (2021). *Pricing: Prinzipien und Prozesse der betrieblichen Preispolitik* (5th ed.). Kohlhammer.

Eggers, F., & Sattler, H. (2011). Preference measurement with conjoint analysis: Overview of state-of-the-art approaches and recent developments. *GfK Marketing Intelligence Review, 3*(1), 36–47.

Gabor, A., & Granger, C. W. (1964). Price sensitivity of the consumer. *Journal of Advertising Research, 4*(4), 40–44.

Kuss, A., Wildner, R., & Kreis, H. (2018). *Marktforschung: Datenerhebung und Datenanalyse*. Springer.

Lewis, R. C., & Shoemaker, S. (1997). Price sensitivity measurement: A tool for the hospitality industry. *Cornell Hotel and Restaurant Administration Quarterly, 38*(2), 44–54.

Lipovetski, S., Magnan, S., & Zanetti-Polzi, A. (2011). Pricing models in marketing research. *Intelligent Information Management, 5*(3), 167–174.

Lyon, D. W. (2002). The price is right (or is it?). *Marketing Research, 14*(4), 8–13.

Powell, C. (2003). The Delphi technique: Myths and realities. *Journal of Advanced Nursing, 41*(4), 376–382.

Reinecke, S., Mühlmeier, S., & Fischer, P. M. (2009). Die van Westendorp-Methode: Ein zu Unrecht vernachlässigtes Verfahren zur Ermittlung der Zahlungsbereitschaft? *Wirtschaftswissenschaftliches Studium: WiSt, 38*(2), 97–100.

Rowe, G., Wright, G., & Bolger, F. (1991). Delphi: A reevaluation of research and theory. *Technological Forecasting and Social Change, 39*(3), 235–251.

Simon, H., & Fassnacht, M. (2016). *Preismanagement: Strategie – Analyse – Entscheidung – Umsetzung* (4th ed.). Springer.

Sullivan, P. (2003). *Comparing price sensitivity research models for new products*. Working Paper, Portland State University.

Van Westendorp, P. H. (1976). *NSS-price sensitivity meter: A new approach to study consumer perception of prices*. Venice ESOMAR Congress, European Marketing Research Society.

Völckner, F. (2006). Methoden zur Messung individueller Zahlungsbereitschaften: Ein Überblick zum State of the Art. *Journal für Betriebswirtschaft, 56*(1), 33–60.

Wildner, R. (2003). Marktforschung für den Preis. *Jahrbuch der Absatz- und Verbrauchsforschung, 49*(2003), 4–26.

6
Auctions

Auctions are a standard method for determining and skimming willingness to pay (Diller and Hermann 2003). The prevalence of auctions has increased with digitalization (Skiera and Spann 2003, p. 625). Well-known examples of online and offline auctions are offered by *Google, eBay, Ricardo.ch, Christie's, Sotheby's, United Charity*, and *MyHammer*. Auctions increase transparency and intensify competition through spatial and temporal compression of the market.

6.1 Significance, Goals, and Fields of Application

In an auction, different bidders independently estimate the value of a product or service. The individual assessments are not public. Finally, the bidder with the highest willingness to pay is awarded the contract. The degree of market consolidation—i.e., the number of bidders—is decisive for the efficiency of an auction. From the supplier's point of view, the number of bidders is particularly decisive. It gives rise to *network effects*: More buyers attract more sellers, and more sellers attract more buyers. The Internet economy increases the importance of auctions for active price management. Especially online, larger marketplaces like *Ricardo.ch* or *eBay* prevail.

Auctions have different objectives (Skiera and Spann 2003): The main aim is to settle transactions. In addition, auctions can be used to conduct market research. Analogous to *conjoint analysis* (see Sect. *5.2.2*), they help to determine willingness to pay. Furthermore, auctions can serve as an effective marketing communication instrument, e.g., auctions of limited editions or unique items. The automobile manufacturer *Ferrari* offers a well-known example: The company auctioned off its latest model, "La Ferrari Aperta," for a hammer price of €8.3 million to benefit the international non-governmental organization *Save the Children*.

Different fields of application can be distinguished (Skiera and Spann 2003). The state, companies, and private individuals act as buyers and sellers. Table 6.1 illustrates possible fields of application and the respective roles of the state, companies, and private individuals:

(a)   *The state as a seller*

Internal public auctions occur between the state as a seller and the *state as a buyer*. Government tenders take place between the state as a seller and *companies as buyers*. One example is mobile communications licenses for 4G and 5G, which have been auctioned off in various countries for billions. Occasionally, the state acts vis-à-vis private individuals, such as in auctions by lost and found offices or confiscated stolen property by the police.

Table 6.1 Fields of application of auctions *(Source: Own presentation updated based on Skiera and Spann 2003)*

	Sellers		
Buyers	State	Company	Private
State	Internal auction of public sector	State tenders	E.g., *my-hammer.de*, *Monster.com*
Company	E.g., 5G licenses	E.g., Google Ads	
Private	Auctions of estates, found objects, stolen goods	E.g., *eBay.com* (new products)	E.g., *Ricardo.ch* (second-hand), charity auctions

(b) *Companies as sellers*

If companies act as sellers and the *state as a buyer*, this is usually done via public tenders. An example of an auction between a company as the seller (*Google*) and buyer companies is *Google Ads'* keywords. Auctions between companies as sellers of new products and *private individuals as buyers* regularly happen on auction platforms like *eBay*.

(c) *Private individuals as sellers*

Private individuals usually act as sellers on auction platforms like *eBay*, *Ricardo.ch*, and *myHammer.de*, or at privately organized charity auctions.

6.2 Auction Forms

Choosing the right auction form—two-sided, open, and hidden—is crucial for the final price.

6.2.1 One and Two-Sided Auctions

While ordinary transactions occur between one buyer and one seller, there must be several parties on at least one of the two sides (buyers or sellers) in auctions. Therefore, a first distinction is made between one-sided and two-sided auctions: In a *forward auction*, there are multiple parties on the buyer's side only. This is the most common auction form. One example is an art or wine auction. In a *reverse auction*, there are multiple parties on the seller's side only. One example is the "Name-Your-Own-Price" auction, where multiple sellers indicate their minimum price and buyers indicate their willingness to pay, for example, for a hotel vacation via the website *priceline.com*. In a *two-sided auction*, there are multiple parties on both sides. Both buyers and sellers can change their bid prices. By continuously bringing the two sides together, this form is concluded quickly. A typical example is securities trading on the stock

Table 6.2 Auctions versus trade *(Source: Own presentation)*

Buyers	Sellers	
	One seller	Multiple sellers
One buyer	Trade (no auction)	Reverse auction
Multiple buyers	Forward auction (common auction form)	Two-sided auction (e.g., securities market)

exchange, where buyers *and* sellers quote a price. Table 6.2 visualizes the auction forms.

6.2.2 Open Auctions

A distinction can be made between *open* and *hidden auctions*. In open auctions, all bids are publicly visible to all participants. This is a classic auction. Typical forms are outlined below.

(a) **English auction**

In the *English auction* (ascending auction), auction participants or the auctioneer raises the price gradually and publicly. All bidders can bid or drop out at any time. The contract is awarded to the bidder who submits the last bid. If bidders drop out of the auction process in case of indifference, the benefit of the highest bidder is always positive (Bannier 2005). For a company, the advantage is to capture the highest individual willingness to pay.

(b) **Japanese auction**

The *Japanese auction* (ascending auction) is a variant of the English auction. The auctioneer raises the price until there is only one bidder left. The advantage is that this auction can be carried out quickly and is suitable for large quantities of goods, for example, in the fish trade.

(c) *Dutch auction*

In the *Dutch auction* (descending auction), the auctioneer starts with a very high price and continuously lowers it during the auction. The winning bid is awarded to the bidder, who is the first to be willing to pay the called price. The benefit of the highest bidder is zero since the bid corresponds precisely to their individual value. The advantage for companies is that it is fast and suitable for selling similar goods, e.g., tulip or tobacco crops (Bannier 2005). Nowadays, many Dutch auctions are conducted electronically.

(d) *American auction*

In the *American auction* (also all-pay auction), each bidder immediately pays the difference between their bid and the previous bid. This form of auction is usually conducted for the benefit of charitable causes, as all—except the last—bidder(s) receive no performance for the bid paid. For example, if a football star's jersey is auctioned off to benefit *Unicef*, each bidder pays $5 for each bid until no one in the room is willing to spend an additional $5 to purchase the jersey. This auction, especially with many bidders, results in very high proceeds in favor of the charity.

(e) *Order auction*

The *order auction* is a particular case. The initiative comes from the buyer, not the seller. Over a longer period, falling bids determine which seller is willing to provide the desired service at the lowest price. The enquirer is usually not obliged to select the offer with the lowest price. In addition to price, other factors such as website presence, ratings, and references can be considered. Examples are the online platforms *MyHammer* and *renovero*. Here, inquirers can post their craft or renovation projects, obtain quotes from professional craftsmen and craftswomen, and then decide on the most suitable offer.

6.2.3 Hidden Auctions

In *sealed-bid auctions,* bids are concealed and invisible to the other auction participants. A distinction is made between *first-* and *second-price auctions.*

(a) ***First-price auction***

In the *first-price auction,* all bidders submit their bids concealed. The winning bid is awarded to the bidder who has stated the highest price. The benefit of the highest bidder is equal to the value of the good minus the price bid. *First-price auctions* are frequently used in awarding government bonds and government construction contracts. They are now also used for *Google Ads*: Here, bidders can specify a *Bid* for the maximum amount they are willing to pay for a click. Multiplying the *Bid* by a *Quality Score* (for relevance, expected click-through rate, and landing page experience) and the *Impact Format* (for the anticipated effect of further advertising on the click-through rate) results in the *Ad Rank*. The bidder with the highest *AdRank* is awarded the contract (see Fig. 6.1).

(b) ***Second-Price Auction***

The *second-price auction,* or *Vickrey auction,* is named after Nobel Prize winner William S. *Vickrey* (1911–1996). All bidders submit their bids

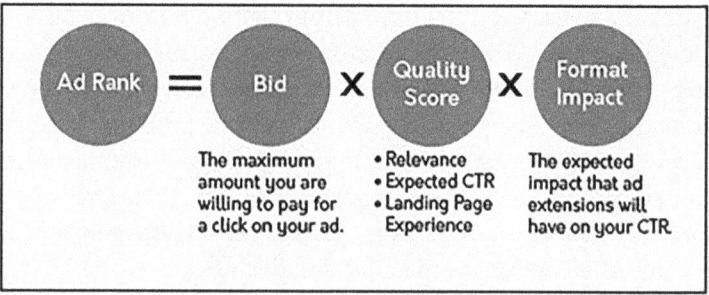

Fig. 6.1 Google Ads: Ad Rank *(Source:* Bochiwal 2017*)*

concealed, and the highest bidder wins the auction. However, the highest bidder does not pay the price of their own bid but the price of the next bid below it. Thus, the benefit of the highest bidder is positive. It is equal to the value of their bid minus the price to be paid (Vickrey 1961). *Second-price auctions* are common in automated processes, such as real-time bidding for online advertising. In the past, *Google* used second-price auctions for Google Ads. The advantage of *second-price auctions* is that bidders quote a higher price than in first-price auctions because if they win, in most cases, they do not have to pay their bid but the lower next bid. This skims off even more willingness to pay.

6.3 Other Design Dimensions

In the following, further possibilities of price management to exploit the potential of auctions are explained (following Skiera and Spann 2003).

(a) *Participating*

As a rule, the more *participants* in auctions, the better. However, under certain circumstances, it may make sense to limit the number of bidders, for example, to reduce risk (e.g., to ensure solvency) or for quality assurance purposes, for example, to ensure that only genuinely interested bidders participate.

(b) *Participation fee or gratuity*

Auction organizers can introduce a *participation fee or bonus*. Fees and bonuses influence the number of bidders: While a participation fee is intended to reduce the number of participants, participation bonuses are intended to encourage additional people to participate.

(c) *Auction duration*

The total *duration of the auction* and the end of the auction can be defined. Thus, auctions can either end at a fixed time (such as an *eBay* auction with a fixed duration, e.g., 24 h) or have a variable end (such as art or wine auctions that continue until no further bids are made).

(d) *Minimum price*

Organizers of auctions or bidders should define the minimum price for an item (e.g., a starting price of €0 on *eBay* for a standard item or a starting price of €200,000 for a classic car auction).

(e) *Binding nature of the commandments*

The *binding nature of the bids* is crucial to the success of an auction.

(f) *Sale of several identical units of one product*

Suppose *several identical units of a product* (e.g., wine or fish) are auctioned. In that case, sellers should weigh the advantages and disadvantages of simultaneous and sequential auctions and decide on one of the two auction forms.

References

Bannier, C. E. (2005). Arten von Auktionen. In *Vertragstheorie* (pp. 201–202). Physica.
Bochiwal, A. (2017, January 2). How to reduce your adwords costs by increasing ad rank and quality score. *LinkedIn.* https://www.linkedin.com/pulse/how-reduce-your-adwords-costs-increasing-ad-rank-quality-bochiwal/
Diller, H., & Hermann, A. (2003). *Handbuch Preispolitik.* Gabler.
Skiera, B., & Spann, M. (2003). Auktionen. In *Handbuch Preispolitik* (pp. 623–641). Gabler.
Vickrey, W. (1961). Counterspeculation, auctions, and competitive sealed tenders. *Journal of Finance, 16*(1), 8–37.

7

Price Management for Business-to-Business Services

In business-to-business markets, active price management is central to increasing profits (Homburg and Totzek 2011). More so, since hardware is currently losing relevance and value creation is shifting toward services. While the monthly wage of a worker has increased from CHF 1200 to 6000 between 1977 and 2019, the price of a drilling machine remained stable at CHF 700 (Hilti internal presentation). Furthermore, decreasing product or hardware margins requires commercializing services. Thus, the need to charge for rising expensive service expenses increases (see Fig. 7.1).

Price management for business-to-business services is characterized by certain special features (Homburg and Totzek 2011; Kienzler and Kowalkowski 2017; Totzek 2011). Essential aspects are (Schmutz 2022):

- Personal relationships between buyers and sellers influence prices.
- Prices are negotiated based on list prices; discounts and bonuses are standard.
- Purchasing, sales, and pricing centers are increasingly professionalized.
- Binding contract terms and large volumes increase the influence of price management on sales.

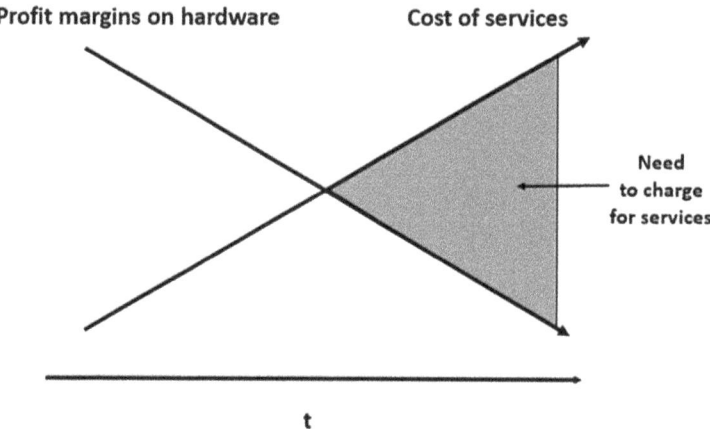

Fig. 7.1 Increasing billing requirements for services *(Source: Own illustration based on* Trachsler 1996*)*

- Lack of information creates uncertainty in price management.
- Supposed market transparency makes price management even more difficult.

Information procurement is a critical challenge in business-to-business price management. To bridge the information gap, and depending on market transparency and information obstacles, information can be obtained through statistics, scientific methods, or networks (ibid., p. 158). However, the increased influence of price management on company sales usually justifies time- and resource-intensive information gathering (ibid., p. 154).

7.1 Industrial Services

The number of industrial services offered by many companies has exploded in recent years. Table 7.1 shows a small selection of services. One reason for the large number of services is increased competition: additional services can be used to compensate for the supposed product or competitive disadvantages. In training courses, sales staff have often

Table 7.1 Industrial services from A to Z *(Source: Reinecke 2021; adapted from Belz and Reinhold 2012)*

Selection of industrial services		
Sales guarantees	Financial aids	Packaging takeback
AI-based services	Warranty services	Software adaptations
Apps	GPS tracking	Special developments
Contract research	Joint venture	Transport organization
Consultations	Customer seminars/specialist lectures	Transport insurance
Chatbot	Marketing automation	Environmental impact assessment
Content marketing	Online support	Value analyses
Customizing	Patent/license agreements	YouTube videos
Data configuration	Personalization	Time studies
Feasibility studies	Recycling/scrapping	....

learned not to offer discounts, but rather to provide additional services. This leads to two challenges: On the one hand, customers' appreciation of the services decreases (because they seem to be offered for free), and on the other hand, services are expensive because they always involve capacity and working time.

Industrial services can be preliminary or ancillary. *Preliminary services* occur in advance of the actual project—for example, the preparation of a detailed quotation. They are challenging to charge for because often no contract has been concluded at this stage. *Ancillary services* include maintenance, service, or recycling supplementary to the main service.

7.2 Clearing Approaches

Clearing approaches are (Reinecke 2019, based on Belz et al. 1991):

1. *Select*
2. *Optimize*
3. *Explain*

4. *Upgrade*
5. *Disconnect*
6. *Let choose*
7. *Transform*

7.2.1 Selection

Selection is about the best possible choice of customers and projects.

It is important to focus on the *respective customer benefit when charging for services*. More precisely, the benefit—the intersection between customer need and product or service—should always be maximized because "[e]very benefit is achieved by a service only if it satisfies a need. [And] [j]ust any part of a service that bypasses parts of needs is only partially useful" (Weinhold-Stünzi 1988). It is, therefore, a matter of covering customer needs as best as possible with one's offering and, at the same time, if possible, not offering an (expensive) reactive service that does not meet a need (see Fig. 7.2).

From a marketing point of view, it is crucial to consider carefully whether customers' needs are met before offering a service. If customer segments or projects do not correspond to the offering, customers are likely to require many expensive additional services—and the probability that customers will not be satisfied remains high. Therefore, the right customer and project selection is one of the most fundamental decisions.

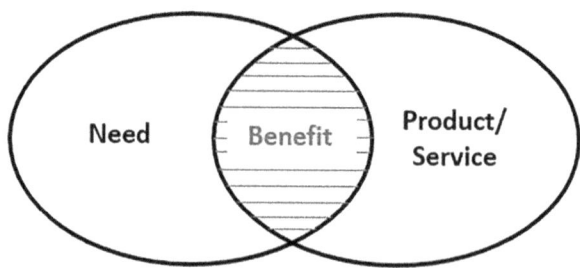

Fig. 7.2 Benefit instead of reactive power *(Source: Own illustration based on Weinhold-Stünzi 1988)*

7.2.2 Optimize

Optimization increases the efficiency of the quotation, for example, through modular quotation systems. On this basis, it is possible to create competent and comprehensive offers for individual customers made up of frequently used standard components. If customers' individual needs are recorded using a checklist, for example, it is possible to put together a personalized offer in a very efficient modular way.

7.2.3 Explain

Services are intangible and invisible. As a result, the willingness to pay is fundamentally lower than that for tangible products. Therefore, services must first be made visible. After all, if customers do not know that a service has been provided, they will not want to pay for it. Transparent communication includes listing each work step on an invoice for maintenance work and, if necessary, having a supervisor check it.

Furthermore, the added value of services must be explained or communicated to customers. For this reason, the focus in *explaining* is on benefit and cost transparency. The goal is customer qualification: to help customers recognize a service's quality and convince them of the added value, for example, through content marketing. Likewise, companies can demonstrate the added value of their services in print and online media (brochures for services, *YouTube videos*, etc.): e.g., how customers recognize the added value of the services, how the company supports them after the purchase, or how the life cycle is accompanied. For example, many US companies have brochures and videos with success stories of their collaboration with customers.

Caterpillar, Dell, and *Hilti* provide valuable examples of how to communicate the added value of their services. *Caterpillar* qualifies its customers via "Caterpillar University," a company-owned website, to optimize the use of their products and services. *Dell* communicates and visualizes the time, cost, and risk savings of "Dell Configuration Services" compared to traditional processes. The cost driver for corporate PCs is often the installation costs, and these can be saved entirely by using *Dell services*.

Hilti had anchored its "added-value philosophy" in its corporate vision for a long time. Since 1941, the company has undergone a complete transformation from a product provider to a service provider: In 1941, it was still purely a product provider. Customers wanted to buy and own *Hilti products*. From 2000, the company requested products on loan. From the customer's point of view, lending, instead of permanent ownership, became more attractive and evolved into Fleet Management. Since 2015, *Hilti* has also been present in *Uber* and *Mobility* cars with ON!Track. ON!Track includes *software* (mainly web and applications), *hardware* (latest technology), and *services* (relevant value-added services such as analysis, execution, and management). ON!Track is billed through pay-per-use (see *Sect. 4.2*).

7.2.4 Upgrade

In upgrading, the goal is to improve the service and charge for the upgrade. For example, customers can be offered two services: one free of charge and one better chargeable service. For instance, a company could offer one free standardized training for ten people at the provider's training center or paid training tailored to the customer's company for 20 people at the customer's headquarters. Another example is sending items by regular mail (free) or express mail (charged).

7.2.5 Separate

Separation involves offering services separately. For example, hardware and service can be separated in the IT area by having two different legal business entities; e.g., *IT Consulting AG* and *IT Hardware AG* issue separate invoices. In this way, hardware and service businesses can also be invoiced separately. The decisive factor is that both companies provide an independent, individually competitive offering. It must, therefore, not be the case that IT Consulting AG only provides services for which only the hardware of IT Hardware AG is suitable.

7.2.6 Let Choose

Customers want to have a choice: In principle, customers choose between a company's offerings and their competition. In the *"let them choose"* approach, the customer's need for choice is already satisfied by one company, for example, by *allowing* them to select different modules or levels. The complexity of the offer should not be too great. Otherwise, customers postpone their decisions. Therefore, even if companies offer choices, they can make clear recommendations. The approach also helps companies whose purchase-deciding needs a supplier cannot yet fully assess. It is also suitable for marketing a large portfolio of services. Suppose an industrial company offers 50 different preliminary and ancillary services. Then, it can communicate that customer companies can use three of these services free of charge when placing an order. The customer company thus chooses three services that provide the highest benefit. At the same time, the company achieves two goals: It introduces the overall service portfolio and communicates that additional services are not free of charge.

7.2.7 Transform

Transforming involves selling benefits instead of hardware. Examples are offerings such as managing a company's entire tool requirements (*Hilti Fleet Management*) or a car subscription via *Clyde* in Switzerland. Ancillary services thus become primary services.

References

Belz, C., & Reinhold, M. (2012). Internationaler Industrievertrieb. In *Internationaler Vertrieb* (pp. 3–222). Springer Gabler.
Belz, C. et al. (1991). *Erfolgreiche Leistungssysteme*. Schäffer.

Homburg, C., & Totzek, D. (2011). *Preismanagement auf Business-to-Business-Märkten*. Gabler.

Kienzler, M., & Kowalkowski, C. (2017). Pricing strategy: A review of 22 years of marketing research. *Journal of Business Research, 78*(May), 101–110.

Schmutz, I. (2022). *Information behavior in B2B pricing. Conceptual development and assessment of managerial strategies in B2B price-relevant information management.* Dissertation, Universität St. Gallen.

Reinecke, S. (2019). Price Management, Lecture Slides, University of St. Gallen, St. Gallen.

Reinecke, S. (2021). Price Management, Lecture Slides, St. Gallen.

Totzek, D. (2011). *Preisverhalten im Wettbewerb* (1st ed.). Gabler Verlag.

Trachsler, S. (1996). *Verrechnung industrieller Dienstleistungen*. Dissertation, University of St. Gallen.

Weinhold-Stünzi, H. (1988). *Marketing in 20 Lektionen*. Fachmed AG.

8

Conclusion on Active Price Management

Price management is a central, strategic, and long-term marketing tool. It is neither tactical nor short-term or operational. It involves actively *shaping, steering, and developing* (Bleicher 2011, p. 46) *prices*. The *price* is more than the number of monetary units a customer must provide to purchase a product. On the one hand, the price must always be considered in the individually perceived *price/performance ratio* or value. On the other hand, price is the third *determinant of profit* alongside costs and sales volume. It has considerable entrepreneurial significance (Reinecke and Hahn 2003, p. 2).

Due to the central entrepreneurial importance of price management, senior executives must deal with it. When delegating price competence, the trade-off between the salesforce's price knowledge (especially regarding existing willingness to pay) and the salesforce's potentially dysfunctional behavior (especially regarding identifying customers with a high willingness to pay) must be considered: Price knowledge argues *for*, and potentially dysfunctional behavior argues *against*, salesforce pricing competence (Joseph 2001; Mishra and Prasad 2004). Specifically, there is a risk that the salesforce will make fewer efforts to attract customers with a high willingness to pay and make price concessions (Stephenson et al.

1979). As a result, corporate profitability declines in the long run. Therefore, a high price competence of the salesforce is only recommended if the search costs for customers are very low or very high (Joseph 2001) or if price controlling fails in viewing the salesforce's existing information on willingness to pay (Mishra and Prasad 2004). Ideally, marketing controlling has access to the salesforce's information about existing willingness to pay to benefit from its price knowledge and avoid dysfunctional behavior.

Before a price management strategy can be defined, the corporate target system must be clarified. More precisely, management must be clear about the target system of safety, growth, and profitability and consciously prioritize these goals. The right strategy depends on the weighting of the above components. This results in the corporate target system (see Fig. 8.1).

Active price managers must observe the following five principles:

1. *Information advantage*

A prerequisite for active price management is price knowledge. For this reason, price managers must gain an *information advantage* over their customers and their competitors. They must always have more price knowledge than others to enforce appropriate prices successfully. In pricing, it must never be the case that customers are better informed than suppliers.

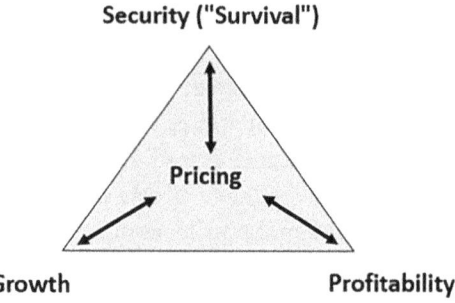

Fig. 8.1 The corporate target system *(Source: Own illustration)*

2. Counterpart Management

Prices *capture* the *value* of offerings. The focus here is on individual customer values. To enforce appropriate prices, companies must create a unique benefit for their customers (*value creation*). Therefore, price *management* also means value creation. The focus should be on the performance in return for the customer. For preliminary and ancillary services, the principle applies: *Never discount labor!* Services involve capacity and working time—and are therefore expensive. Economies of scale can only be achieved to a limited extent for services, so discounts should not be granted wherever possible.

3. Price Differentiation

Price differentiation can exploit different willingness to pay in different customer segments. In this way, an additional contribution margin can be generated. Price differentiation is crucial because it opens up the scope for price management. However, it also has limits, such as internal complexity and customer confusion. Moreover, some forms of price differentiation are prohibited for ethical reasons.

4. Strategic Marketing

Following the traditional St. Gallen management definition, price management is understood as the active *shaping, steering, and development* (Bleicher 2011, p. 46) of *prices*. Price is not purely tactical but a *central strategic marketing instrument: price* changes have an immediate effect and are immediately reflected in the demand and profit of a company.

5. Price image

Whether a price is perceived as fair and accepted depends on the subjective perception of customers. Justified motives and transparent prices are decisive for perceived price fairness and (re)purchasing behavior.

Therefore, it is not the actual price but the perceived price that ultimately decides—and thus the *price image*.

References

Bleicher, K. (2011). *Das Konzept integriertes Management: Visionen – Missionen – Programme*. Campus Verlag.
Joseph, K. (2001). On the optimality of delegating pricing authority to the sales force. *Journal of Marketing, 65*(1), 62–70.
Mishra, B. K., & Prasad, A. (2004). Centralized pricing versus delegating pricing to the salesforce under information asymmetry. *Marketing Science, 23*(1), 21–27.
Reinecke, S., & Hahn, S. (2003). Preisplanung. In H. Diller & A. Herrmann (Eds.), *Handbuch Preispolitik* (pp. 333–355). Springer.
Stephenson, R. P., Cron, W. L., & Frazier, G. L. (1979). Delegating pricing authority to the salesforce: The effects of sales and profit performance. *Journal of Marketing, 43*(1), 21–28.

References

Adida, E. (2021). Outcome-based pricing for new pharmaceuticals via rebates. *Management Science, 67*(2), 892–913.

Amaral, J. V., & Guerreiro, R. (2019). Factors explaining a cost-based pricing essence. *Journal of Business & Industrial Marketing, 34*(8), 1850–1865.

Anderson, E. T., & Simester, D. I. (2004). Long-run effects of promotion depth on new versus established customers: Three field studies. *Marketing Science, 23*(1), 4–20.

Armstrong, M., & Vickers, J. (2010). Competitive non-linear pricing and bundling. *The Review of Economic Studies, 77*(1), 30–60.

Assael, H. (1993). *Marketing principles and strategy*. Thomson Learning.

Backhaus, K., Erichson, B., Gensler, S., Weiber, R., & Weiber, T. (2021). Conjoint-analyse. In *Multivariate Analysemethoden* (pp. 577–653). Springer Gabler.

Balasubramanian, S., Bhattacharya, S., & Krishnan, V. V. (2015). Pricing information goods: A strategic analysis of the selling and pay-per-use mechanisms. *Marketing Science, 34*(2), 218–234.

Bannier, C. E. (2005). Arten von Auktionen. In *Vertragstheorie* (pp. 201–202). Physica.

Becker, J. (2019). *Marketing-Konzeption: Grundlagen des zielstrategischen und operativen Marketing-Managements*. Vahlen.

References

Belz, C. (1991). *Erfolgreiche Leistungssysteme-Anleitung und Beispiele*. Schäffer.

Belz, C., & Schindler, H. (1994). Markeintritt des Mediamarkts in die Schweiz. In C. Belz & T. Tomczak (Eds.), *Preisagressive Fachmärkte – Revolution im schweizerischen Einzelhandel* (pp. 14–39). Research Institute for Sales and Trade.

Belz, C., & Mühlmeier, J. (2000). *International price management [International pricing]: Strategy, price harmonization, tools, case studies*. Ueberrether.

Belz, C., & Reinhold, M. (2012). Internationaler Industrievertrieb. In *Internationaler Vertrieb* (pp. 3–222). Springer Gabler.

Belz, C. et al. (1991). *Erfolgreiche Leistungssysteme*. Schäffer.

Bleicher, K. (2011). *Das Konzept integriertes Management: Visionen – Missionen – Programme*. Campus Verlag.

Bochiwal, A. (2017, January 2). How to reduce your adwords costs by increasing ad rank and quality score. *LinkedIn*. https://www.linkedin.com/pulse/how-reduce-your-adwords-costs-increasing-ad-rank-quality-bochiwal/

Bolton, L. E., Warlop, L., & Alba, J. W. (2003). Consumer perceptions of price (un)fairness. *Journal of Consumer Research, 29*(4), 474–491.

Breidert, C., Hahsler, M., & Reutterer, T. (2006). A review of methods for measuring willingness-to-pay. *Innovative Marketing, 2*(4), 8–32.

Brühwiler, C. (1989). *Der ruinöse Preiskampf: Marketinglösungen bei übersteigertem Wettbewerb*. Dissertation, University of St. Gallen.

Burgernomics: The Big Mac index. (2021, July 21). *The Economist*. https://www.economist.com/big-mac-index

Chyi, H. I. (2005). Willingness to pay for online news: An empirical study on the viability of the subscription model. *Journal of Media Economics, 18*(2), 131–142.

Cross, J. (2021, September 14). iPhone 12: Buy now or wait? *Macworld*. https://www.macworld.com/article/352162/iphone-12-pro-buy-or-wait-specs-price.html

Danaher, P. J. (2002). Optimal pricing of new subscription services: Analysis of a market experiment. *Marketing Science, 21*(2), 119–138.

Derdenger, T., & Kumar, V. (2013). The dynamic effects of bundling as a product strategy. *Marketing Science, 32*(6), 827–859.

Diller, H., & Hermann, A. (2003). *Handbuch Preispolitik*. Gabler.

Diller, H. (2008). Price fairness. *Journal of Product & Brand Management, 17*(5), 353–355.

Diller, H., Beinert, M., Ivens, B., & Müller, S. (2021). *Pricing: Prinzipien und Prozesse der betrieblichen Preispolitik* (5th ed.). Kohlhammer.

Dixit, A., Braunsberger, K., Zinkhan, G. M., & Pan, Y. (2005). Information technology: Enhanced pricing strategies: Managerial and public policy implications. *Journal of Business Research, 58*(9), 1169–1177.

Donaghy, K., McMahon, U., & McDowell, D. (1995). Yield management: An overview. *International Journal of Hospitality Management, 14*(2), 139–150.

Eggers, F., & Sattler, H. (2011). Preference measurement with conjoint analysis: Overview of state-of-the-art approaches and recent developments. *GfK Marketing Intelligence Review, 3*(1), 36–47.

Ellison, G. (2005). A model of add-on pricing. *The Quarterly Journal of Economics, 120*(2), 585–637.

Fassnacht, M. (2003). Preisdifferenzierung. In *Handbuch Preispolitik* (pp. 483–502). Gabler.

Frey, B. S., & Pommerehne, W. W. (1993). On the fairness of pricing – An empirical survey among the general population. *Journal of Economic Behavior & Organization, 20*(3), 295–307.

Froböse, M. (2016). Strategische Marketing-Planung. In *Marketing* (pp. 59–88). Springer Gabler.

Gabor, A., & Granger, C. W. (1964). Price sensitivity of the consumer. *Journal of Advertising Research, 4*(4), 40–44.

Gronholdt, L., Martensen, A., & Kristensen, K. (2000). The relationship between customer satisfaction and loyalty: Cross-industry differences. *Total Quality Management, 11*(4–6), 509–514.

Grosse-Oetringhaus, W. F. (2013). *Strategische Identität – Orientierung im Wandel: Ganzheitliche Transformation zu Spitzenleistungen*. Springer.

Gu, X., Kannan, P. K., & Ma, L. (2018). Selling the premium in freemium. *Journal of Marketing, 82*(6), 10–27.

Hermann, A. (2003). Relevanz des Preismanagements für den Unternehmenserfolg. In *Handbuch Preispolitik* (pp. 33–45). Gabler.

Hermann, A., Xia, L., Monroe, K. B., & Huber, K. (2007). The influence of price fairness on customer satisfaction: An empirical test in the context of automobile purchases. *Journal of Product & Brand Management, 16*(1), 49–58.

Hinterhuber, A. (2008). Customer value-based pricing strategies: Why companies resist. *Journal of Business Strategy, 29*(4), 41–50.

Hinterhuber, A., & Bertini, M. (2011). Profiting when customers choose value over price. *Business Strategy Review, 22*(1), 46–49.

Hinterhuber, A., & Liozu, S. (2012). Is it time to rethink your pricing strategy? *MIT Sloan Management Review, 53*(4), 69–77.

Homburg, C., & Totzek, D. (2011). *Preismanagement auf Business-to-Business-Märkten*. Gabler.

Hu, Y., Shin, J., & Tang, Z. (2012). *Performance-based pricing models in online advertising: Cost per click versus cost per action*. Georgia Institute.

Indounas, K. A. (2009). Successful industrial service pricing. *Journal of Business & Industrial Marketing, 24*(2), 86–97.

Ingenbleek, P. T. (2007). Value-informed pricing in its organizational context: Literature review, conceptual framework, and directions for future research. *Journal of Product & Brand Management, 16*(7), 441–458.

Ingenbleek, P. T. (2014). The theoretical foundations of value-informed pricing in the service-dominant logic of marketing. *Management Decision, 52*(1), 33–53.

Ingenbleek, P. T., Debruyne, M., Frambach, R. T., & Verhallen, T. M. (2003). Successful new product pricing practices: A contingency approach. *Marketing Letters, 14*(4), 289–305.

Joseph, K. (2001). On the optimality of delegating pricing authority to the sales force. *Journal of Marketing, 65*(1), 62–70.

Kahneman, D., & Tversky, A. (1979). Prospect theory: An analysis of decision under risk. *Econometrica, 47*(2), 263–292.

Kienzler, M., & Kowalkowski, C. (2017). Pricing strategy: A review of 22 years of marketing research. *Journal of Business Research, 78*(May), 101–110.

Kienzler, M. (2018). Value-based pricing and cognitive biases: An overview for business markets. *Industrial Marketing Management, 68*, 86–94.

Kim, J. Y., Natter, M., & Spann, M. (2009). Pay what you want: A new participative pricing mechanism. *Journal of Marketing, 73*(1), 44–58.

Konuk, F. A. (2018). Price fairness, satisfaction, and trust as antecedents of purchase intentions toward organic food. *Journal of Consumer Behavior, 17*(2), 141–148.

Kotler, P., Keller, K. L., & Bliemel, F. (2007). *Marketing-Management: Strategien für wertschaffendes Handeln* (12th updated and revised edition). Pearson Studies.

Kübler, R., Seifert, R., & Kandziora, M. (2021). Content valuation strategies for digital subscription platforms. *Journal of Cultural Economics, 45*, 295–326.

Kucher, E. (1985). Preisresponsedynamik: Theorie und Messung. In *Scannerdaten und Preissensitivität bei Konsumgütern* (pp. 88–206). Gabler.

Kumar, V. (2014). Making "freemium" work. *Harvard Business Review, 92*(5), 27–29.

References

Kuss, A., Wildner, R., & Kreis, H. (2018). *Marktforschung: Datenerhebung und Datenanalyse*. Springer.

Lewis, R. C., & Shoemaker, S. (1997). Price sensitivity measurement: A tool for the hospitality industry. *Cornell Hotel and Restaurant Administration Quarterly, 38*(2), 44–54.

Lipovetski, S., Magnan, S., & Zanetti-Polzi, A. (2011). Pricing models in marketing research. *Intelligent Information Management, 5*(3), 167–174.

Lyon, D. W. (2002). The price is right (or is it?). *Marketing Research, 14*(4), 8–13.

Malc, D., Selinšek, A., Dlačić, J., & Milfelner, B. (2021). Exploring the emotional side of price fairness perceptions and its consequences. *Economic Research, 34*(1), 1931–1948.

Marburger, D. (2012). *Innovative pricing strategies to increase profits*. Business Expert Press.

Marn, M. V., Roegner, E. V., & Zawada, C. C. (2003). The power of pricing. *The McKinsey Quarterly, 2003*(1), 26–36.

Maxwell, S. (2002). Rule-based price fairness and its effect on willingness to purchase. *Journal of Economic Psychology, 23*(2), 191–212.

McCarthy, E. J. (1960). *Basic marketing: A managerial approach*. Homewood.

Meffert, H., Burmann, C., Kirchgeorg, M., & Eisenbeiss, M. (2018). *Marketing: Grundlagen marktorientierter Unternehmensführung Konzepte – Instrumente – Praxisbeispiele*. Springer.

Michel, S. (2014). Capture more value. *Harvard Business Review, 92*(10), 20.

Michel, S., & Pfäffli, P. (2013). Obstacles to implementing value-based pricing. *Perspectives for Managers, 185*, 1–4.

Mishra, B. K., & Prasad, A. (2004). Centralized pricing versus delegating pricing to the salesforce under information asymmetry. *Marketing Science, 23*(1), 21–27.

Monroe, K. B. (2003). *Pricing-making profitable decisions* (3rd ed.). McGraw Hill/Irwin.

Mortimer, G. (2019). The decoy effect: How you are influenced to choose without really knowing it. *The Conversation*, 1–6.

Nagle, T. T., Hogan, J., & Zale, J. (2011). *The strategy and tactics of pricing: A guide to growing more profitably*. Prentice Hall.

Piercy, N. F., Cravens, D. W., & Lane, N. (2010). Thinking strategically about pricing decisions. *The Journal of Business Strategy, 31*(5), 38–48.

Powell, C. (2003). The Delphi technique: Myths and realities. *Journal of Advanced Nursing, 41*(4), 376–382.

Reinecke, S. (1996). Management von IT-Outsourcing-Kooperationen: *Marketing für komplexe Informationstechnologie-Dienstleistungen.* Dissertation, University of St. Gallen.
Reinecke, S. (2019). Price Management, Lecture Slides, University of St. Gallen, St. Gallen.
Reinecke, S. (2021). Price Management, Lecture Slides, St. Gallen.
Reinecke, S., & Hahn, S. (2003). Preisplanung. In H. Diller & A. Herrmann (Eds.), *Handbuch Preispolitik* (pp. 333–355). Springer.
Reinecke, S., Fischer, P. M., & Mühlmeier, S. (2008). Aktuelle Herausforderungen für das Preiscontrolling. *Controlling & Management, 52*(2), 112–114.
Reinecke, S., Mühlmeier, S., & Fischer, P. M. (2009). Die van Westendorp-Methode: Ein zu Unrecht vernachlässigtes Verfahren zur Ermittlung der Zahlungsbereitschaft? *Wirtschaftswissenschaftliches Studium: WiSt, 38*(2), 97–100.
Rowe, G., Wright, G., & Bolger, F. (1991). Delphi: A reevaluation of research and theory. *Technological Forecasting and Social Change, 39*(3), 235–251.
Sato, S. (2019). Freemium as optimal menu pricing. *International Journal of Industrial Organization, 63*, 480–510
Schindler, H. (1998). *Marktorientiertes Preismanagement.* Schindler.
Schmidt, K. M., Spann, M., & Zeithammer, R. (2015). Pay what you want as a marketing strategy in monopolistic and competitive markets. *Management Science, 61*(6), 1217–1236.
Schmutz, I. (2022). *Information behavior in B2B pricing. Conceptual development and assessment of managerial strategies in B2B price-relevant information management.* Dissertation, Universität St. Gallen.
Schüwer, U., & Kosfeld, M. (2010). *Add-on pricing, consumer myopia and regulatory intervention.* ZBW.
Seufert, E. B. (2014). *Freemium economics: Leveraging analytics and user segmentation to drive revenue.* Elsevier.
Shapiro, B. P. (1968). Psychology of pricing. *Harvard Business Review, 46*(4), 14.
Shapiro, B. P. (2002, July 22). *Is performance-based pricing the right price for you?.* Harvard Business School. https://hbswk.hbs.edu/item/is-performance-based-pricing-the-right-price-for-you
Shapiro, B. P. (2003, February 10). *Commodity busters: Be a price maker, not a price taker.* Harvard Business School. https://hbswk.hbs.edu/item/commodity-busters-be-a-price-maker-not-a-price-taker
Shipley, D., & Jobber, D. (2001). Integrative pricing via the pricing wheel. *Industrial Marketing Management, 30*(3), 301–314.

Siems, F. (2009). *Preismanagement: Konzepte – Strategien – Instrumente*. Vahlens Handbücher.
Simon, H. (1979). Dynamische Erklärungen des Nachfragerverhaltens aus Carryover-Effekt und Responsefunktion. In *Consumer Behavior and Information* (pp. 415–444). Gabler.
Simon, H. (1992). *Price management: Analysis-strategy-implementation* (2nd ed.). Springer.
Simon, H., & Fassnacht, M. (2016). *Preismanagement: Strategie – Analyse – Entscheidung – Umsetzung* (4th ed.). Springer.
Simon, H., & Fassnacht, M. (2019). *Price management: Strategy – analysis – decision – implementation*. Springer.
Simon, H. (2020). *Am Gewinn ist noch keine Firma kaputt gegangen*. Campus.
Skiera, B., & Spann, M. (2003). Auktionen. In *Handbuch Preispolitik* (pp. 623–641). Gabler.
Skiera, B., & Lambrecht, A. (2006). Flat rate versus pay-per-use pricing. In *Turbulence in the telecommunications and media industry* (pp. 77–101). Springer.
Steinert-Threlkeld, T. (1993): Pricing approach sets company apart, in: The Dallas Morning News, "EDS: The Next Horizon.", Dallas, Texas, pp. 44–45.
Stephenson, R. P., Cron, W. L., & Frazier, G. L. (1979). Delegating pricing authority to the salesforce: The effects of sales and profit performance. *Journal of Marketing, 43*(1), 21–28.
Sullivan, P. (2003). *Comparing price sensitivity research models for new products*. Working Paper, Portland State University.
Sun, B. (2005). Promotion effect on endogenous consumption. *Marketing Science, 24*(3), 430–443.
Tacke, G. (2013). *Nichtlineare Preisbildung: Höhere Gewinne durch Differenzierung* (Vol. 64). Springer.
Tomczak, T., Kuss, A., & Reinecke, S. (2014). *Marketingplanung*. Springer Gabler.
Tomczak, T., Reinecke, S., & Kuss, A. (2017). *Strategic marketing: Market-oriented corporate and business unit planning*. Springer.
Tomczak, T., Reinecke, S., & Kuss, A. (2018): *Strategic Marketing. Market-Oriented Corporate and Business-Unit Planning*. Springer-Gabler.
Totzek, D. (2011). *Preisverhalten im Wettbewerb* (1st ed.). Gabler Verlag.
Trachsler, S. (1996). *Verrechnung industrieller Dienstleistungen*. Dissertation, University of St. Gallen.
Tucker, S. A. (1966). *Pricing for higher profit: Criteria, methods, applications*. McGraw-Hill.

Van Westendorp, P. H. (1976). *NSS-price sensitivity meter: A new approach to study consumer perception of prices.* Venice ESOMAR Congress, European Marketing Research Society.

Vickrey, W. (1961). Counterspeculation, auctions, and competitive sealed tenders. *Journal of Finance, 16*(1), 8–37.

Vinod, B. (2021). *The evolution of yield management in the airline industry.* Springer.

Völckner, F. (2006). Methoden zur Messung individueller Zahlungsbereitschaften: Ein Überblick zum State of the Art. *Journal für Betriebswirtschaft, 56*(1), 33–60.

Weinhold-Stünzi, H. (1988). *Marketing in 20 Lektionen.* Fachmed AG.

Weinhold-Stünzi, H. (1994). *Marketing in 20 Lektionen.* Fachmed

Wildner, R. (2003). Marktforschung für den Preis. *Jahrbuch der Absatz- und Verbrauchsforschung, 49*(2003), 4–26.

Wu, C., & Cosguner, K. (2020). Profiting from the decoy effect: A case study of an online diamond retailer. *Marketing Science, 39*(5), 974–995.

Wübker, S. (2006). *Power Pricing für Banken: Wege aus der Ertragskrise.* Campus.

Xia, L., Monroe, K. B., & Cox, J. L. (2004). The Price is Unfair! A conceptual framework of price fairness perceptions. *Journal of Marketing, 68*(4), 1–15.

Zeithammer, R., & Liu, P. (2006). *When is auctioning preferred to posting a fixed selling price?* University of Chicago.

Zhang, B. (2012). Capacity-constrained multiple-market price discrimination. *Computers & Operations Research, 39*(1), 105–111.

Zhang, M., & Bell, P. (2012). Price fencing in the practice of revenue management: An overview and taxonomy. *Journal of Revenue and Pricing Management, 11*(2), 146–159.

Zhou, J. (2017). Competitive bundling. *Econometrica, 85*(1), 145–172.

Zielke, S. (2007). Bestimmungsfaktoren der Preisfairness von Lebensmitteldiscountern. *Marketing Review St. Gallen, 24*(4), 17–20.

GPSR Compliance
The European Union's (EU) General Product Safety Regulation (GPSR) is a set of rules that requires consumer products to be safe and our obligations to ensure this.

If you have any concerns about our products, you can contact us on

ProductSafety@springernature.com

In case Publisher is established outside the EU, the EU authorized representative is:

Springer Nature Customer Service Center GmbH
Europaplatz 3
69115 Heidelberg, Germany

www.ingramcontent.com/pod-product-compliance
Lightning Source LLC
LaVergne TN
LVHW041204250326
834689LV00001BA/3